History Skills

D0571314

Degree-level history is characterised, not only by knowledge and understanding of the human past, but by a battery of skills and qualities which are as directly applicable to employment as to professional postgraduate training or academic research. *History Skills* gives frank and practical help to students throughout their university course with advice on:

- research methods
- taking notes
- participating in class
- coursework
- examinations
- the dissertation.

Designed as a guide to success, the book helps to develop the critical skills that students need to get the most out of their course.

This second edition has been thoroughly updated to take into account digital resources and the benefits and risks associated with online research. New chapters on the first-year experience and employability help students to adjust to the way history is taught at university and explore the opportunities available to them after graduating.

Offering an unrivalled 'insider's view' of what it takes to succeed, *History Skills* provides a comprehensive toolkit for all history students.

Mary Abbott is Principal Lecturer in History at Anglia Ruskin University. Her previous publications include *Family Ties* (1993), *Life Cycles in England 1560–1720* (1996) and *Family Affairs: A history of the family in 20th century England* (2003). She is a member of the Higher Education Academy's History Advisory Panel.

History Skills

A Student's Handbook

Second edition

Edited by Mary Abbott

Routledge
Taylor & Francis Group

LONDON AND NEW YORK

First published 1996
by Routledge

This edition published 2009
by Routledge
2 Park Square, Milton Park, Abingdon, Oxon OX14 4RN

Simultaneously published in the USA and Canada
by Routledge
270 Madison Ave, New York, NY 10016

*Routledge is an imprint of the Taylor & Francis Group,
an informa business*

Typeset in Helvetica and Times New Roman by
Florence Production Ltd, Stoodleigh, Devon
Printed and bound in Great Britain by
The Cromwell Press, Trowbridge, Wiltshire

British Library Cataloguing in Publication Data
A catalogue record for this book is available
from the British Library

Library of Congress Cataloging in Publication Data
History skills: a student's handbook / edited by
    Mary Abbott. – 2nd ed.
        p. cm.
    1. History–Study and teaching (Higher)–United States.
    2. History–Research. I. Abbott, Mary, 1942–
    D16.3.H54 2008
    907.1'173–dc22   2008005593

ISBN10: 0–415–46691–1 (hbk)
ISBN10: 0–415–46690–3 (pbk)
ISBN10: 0–203–89266–6 (ebk)

ISBN13: 978–0–415–46691–2 (hbk)
ISBN13: 978–0–415–46690–5 (pbk)
ISBN13: 978–0–203–89266–4 (ebk)

Contents

Contributors

Dr Mary Abbott has taught History undergraduates for over 30 years. As her university's representative in an Access Validating Agency, she is familiar with an important alternative route into Higher Education for non-traditional students. She is a member of the Higher Education Academy's History Advisory Panel. Mary Abbott makes significant use of visual and material evidence in her teaching.

Dr Adrian Gregory lectures in Modern History at the University of Oxford.

Penny King is a university Academic Liaison Librarian with responsibility for History. She provides training and support for students at every stage of their academic career.

Tony Kirby has taught History undergraduates for over 30 years. His passion is the history of railways; his roles as officer in the Cambridge Antiquarian Society and the Cambridgeshire Record Society illustrate his wider interests in the history of material culture and in archival research. Tony Kirby has devised and practised an innovative and very popular style of group supervision of undergraduate dissertations.

Dr Seán Lang was Head of History at Hills Road VI Form College in Cambridge for ten years. There he prepared students to survive and thrive in Higher Education. Recently both Government and Opposition have consulted him on the redesign of the 14–19 History curriculum. Seán Lang produced the supplementary text for the fourth edition of John Tosh's *Pursuit of History*.

Dr Susan O'Brien taught in modern universities before moving into academic leadership at Liverpool Hope and, as Pro Vice-Chancellor, at the University of Staffordshire; she is now Principal of the Lady Margaret Beaufort Institute, Cambridge.

1 The first-year experience

Seán Lang

Embarking on university study has always been exciting and disorientating in almost equal measure. The celebrated eighteenth-century historian Edward Gibbon went up to Oxford full of high hopes only to find that his tutors took no interest in him beyond the rather vague recommendation that 'You must read.' He left Oxford after 14 months, looking back on his time as 'the most idle and unprofitable of my whole life'. University life has changed a lot since then, but it is still the case that many students risk Gibbonian levels of disappointment by arriving with only a vague notion of what to expect of university and what will be expected of them.

What is a university?

A university is not a school. Although, confusingly, the word 'school' is used in universities, as an alternative to 'faculty' or 'department', as in 'School of Education' or to denote trends in thinking, as in 'the revisionist school', or sometimes as a technical term for final examinations, university and school in the normal sense of the word are two very different institutions and experiences. Schools are heavily influenced by the examination boards that devise courses, set exam papers, draw up the mark schemes and mark the examination scripts. Universities have a significantly different history. In the Middle Ages they were self-sufficient communities of scholars. Their purpose was to study the world and, by so doing, to both extend the sum of human knowledge and learn more of the workings of God. The gowns and hoods worn at university graduation ceremonies are a reminder of universities' medieval origins. So is the concept of academic freedom.

One of the biggest differences between school and university is that lecturers do not have to guess what will be on the exam papers, since they set and mark them – overseen by External Examiners who ensure that standards are maintained. Many first-year courses, which often introduce students to broad themes such as 'western civilisation', are designed and assessed centrally. Second- and, particularly, third-year topics usually relate to the areas of the lecturers' own research. This close relationship between research and teaching can be very fruitful: there is an undeniable 'buzz' to be had from working close to the cutting edge of research. It also represents a fundamental difference between the experiences of school and university.

Teachers and students

The relationship between university lecturers and students is very different from that between teachers and pupils in school. Under-graduates are subject to university rules governing attendance, submitting work, conduct and so on, but they are also adults; indeed, some of them are mature students who are older than their lecturers. This does not just mean that students enjoy the liberty to drink or smoke; it is a sign of a fundamentally different learning relationship. Universities do not offer lessons. A school lesson, if it is well planned, is a varied, interactive learning session, with a balance between explanation from the teacher, questions from pupils, group work and other activities. But the teacher retains at all times a role of leadership and authority, however lightly it might be worn. A university lecture, by contrast, is a set-piece performance, where the lecturer speaks for about an hour. A gifted lecturer can so enthral an audience that the subject comes alive and the hour flies by; not all lecturers, however, are gifted, as generations of students will confirm. A seminar is a smaller discussion group, for which it is usually necessary to prepare by reading materials or by writing a paper. A tutorial is a meeting between a lecturer and one or two students, generally to offer individual support. You can expect to encounter any or all of these in your first year of university study.

Experience, supported by research, suggests that most A level students look to their teachers to give them 'the facts', wrapped up in as much clear explanation as possible. Teachers will certainly try to make sure that their lessons cover everything that might come up in the exam. Such is the pressure to get through the course that they may feel obliged to exclude anything else, however interesting. There is no obvious equivalent of this sort of lesson in university teaching and learning. A good lecture can certainly explain key concepts and give examples to illustrate them, but there is no sense in which even a whole course of lectures is expected or designed to 'get you through the exam'. Students are expected to see lectures as a starting point for reading far more widely. No lecturer is impressed by an examination script that consists entirely of material given in lectures, especially if he or she originally gave them. In seminars and tutorials, the lecturers assume students already know the outline of facts and events; there is no question of stopping the discussion to teach them.

At the same time, it is expected that students will speak out and challenge both each other and the lecturer. This can be daunting with people with 'Dr' and 'Professor' in front of their names who may have written important books on the subject under discussion, but it is important not to be overawed by academic titles or distinction: university is about a learning partnership *between* lecturer and student; it is not about the student being taught *by* the lecturer.

From school history to university history

For a complex set of interconnected reasons the school history curriculum has become very narrow in recent years. Not only do pupils study fewer topics than in the past, but there has also been a marked tendency to repeat topics at different levels. The most notorious example is the study of Nazi Germany, which often comes up in English schools in each year from Year 9 to Year 13. Students coming to university straight from school or college should appreciate that they have so far only scratched the surface of what history has to offer, in terms of period, geographical area, and type of study. Some universities address this by obliging students to study unfamiliar periods in their first year; students who were grappling with Hitler's foreign policy for A level in the summer might thus find themselves getting their heads round eighteenth-century Whigs and Tories or Anglo-Saxon saints and kings by Christmas. It is important to see this as an opportunity to widen historical horizons: new periods are no more intrinsically 'difficult' than familiar ones and opting to study the same topics at university as you studied at school does not make for a good historical education and is a poor preparation for the outside world. A good historian may know lots about a little, but the best historians know lots about lots.

Is university history harder than school history?

An Advanced or Higher level qualification in history is not generally required of applicants to university courses in the subject. Understandably, those coming to university history without having done the subject at school can feel at a disadvantage, especially if the first-year course overlaps with topics other students in the class covered recently. Any disadvantage seldom lasts long, however, and is certainly not reflected either in how such 'non-A level' students cope on university history courses or in their final results. Indeed, it could be argued that having studied a period at school can lead the unwary student into overconfidence.

There is, inevitably, much talk of a 'leap' or 'step' up from A level or history Highers to university history. It is undoubtedly true – and right – that university history is more demanding than school history. The gap is in fact quite manageable, but some important features of university history can throw the first-year student who is not expecting them. At first, many aspects of university history might seem familiar, even if the period you are studying is a new one: after all, power politics or social problems such as poverty or crime operated in much the same way at different periods of history. Lectures may be different in format from lessons, but there is the same talk of sources and evidence and the need for wider reading that you will be familiar with from school or college. However, underneath this superficial similarity lurks a major difference, though it may take a week or so to sink in: at university students are expected to take command of their own learning.

It is often only in the first year of university that many undergraduates come to realise the extent to which they were spoon-fed at school. Publishers produce books and resources tied ever more closely to the specific requirements of particular exam courses, badged with the exam board logo and often written by a senior examiner. Teachers often identify exactly which pages, even which paragraphs and sentences, students need to read. Although many A level students learn about different historians' opinions or theories, very few actually read more than a few lines on a teacher's handout of what these people actually wrote. Indeed, few A level history students use any books that were not specifically designed for A level study – the very different situation at university can therefore come as something of a culture shock. Students' guides and textbooks are certainly available but, since each university designs its own curriculum, they cannot be as closely aligned to the specific requirements of a particular course as A level resources are. In any case, lecturers expect students to read much more widely and to do so without being prompted.

I deal with how best to respond to this exhortation to read (one aspect of university life that has not changed since Gibbon's time) later in this chapter.

A similar surprise can await students among the historical sources. You will certainly have done source papers at school but, unless you have undertaken an Individual Study (a piece of research undertaken by a student working alone), it is unlikely that you will actually have worked with any *real* historical sources, even in transcription. At university, historical sources come in the shape of whole documents or books that you will find yourself required to read. This can come as a bit of a shock after the neatly packaged source extracts used at Advanced and Higher level. Many sources are in foreign languages. Few universities have a formal requirement for history students to read foreign languages, but it is well worth your honing any language skills you may have. Facility with a language is highly appreciated in undergraduates, not least because it is so relatively rare. If, once you have graduated, you decide to do a research degree involving foreign countries or cultures, you will be expected to master the relevant language or languages (and for English history topics earlier than about 1700 this includes Latin).

Perhaps the most important attribute to develop, however, is a sense of genuine historical awareness and curiosity going well beyond the strict boundaries of your course. You should certainly make time to visit museums, galleries and historic sites near your campus. If there is an exhibition on a topic directly relevant to your course it is doubly important to go. After all, it may feature in the next assessment. Similarly, it is important to keep an eye and ear open for relevant history programmes on television and radio. It can be hard to keep up with historical literature on top of the reading required for your course, but there are plenty of useful shortcuts. *History Today*, *BBC History Magazine*, which appear monthly, and the weekend quality newspapers all carry book reviews that often take the form of a short essay on the book's subject; *The Times Higher Education Supplement* and *The Times Literary Supplement* also carry reviews and historical articles and offer a painless way to keep up to date. Book reviews in academic journals are aimed at a university readership; the broadest selections are those in *History* and the *Annual Bulletin of Historical Literature*, both published by the Historical Association.

Learning and working

University learning has changed considerably in recent years, taking many of its cues from practice in schools. Once students were fed a fairly unvaried diet of essay tasks; now it is common for first-year undergraduates to be set smaller assignments such as reports on visits to historic sites or book reviews, often as a way of building up towards essay writing. Seminar contributions and PowerPoint presentations are similarly working their way into the pattern of assessment. Various aspects of these different forms of work are dealt with elsewhere in this book; here I want to stress two points: note-taking and referencing.

Note-taking

Advice on note-taking has become a virtual industry. Study skills tutors will offer you advice on mind maps, spider diagrams, flow charts and many other ways of note-taking. Sometimes students can feel a bit harried by this. Let me say at once that I for one have never been able to use or follow a spider diagram and it has not yet held me back either in my historical understanding or in my career. You, however, may find a spider diagram matches your way of thinking perfectly. Whichever method you adopt, it is important to be aware that note-taking serves two different purposes, and you need to deal with both of them.

The first purpose is to help fix the details in the mind of the note-taker. At this point someone usually cracks a joke about a lecture being the transfer of information from the lecturer's notes to the student's without passing through the mind of either, but this has never been entirely fair. The mere act of writing something down can help it to lodge in the brain. However, there is a huge difference between taking notes on a new topic and on a topic you already know. In the latter case you need only note down things that are new to you; indeed you may not need to write anything down at all.

The second purpose of note-taking is to provide a basis for writing assignments or revising for exams, possibly many months later. If you are planning to refer to your notes later, do not leave it until 'later' to get them into an easily usable form. Typing them up will make it easer for you to cross-reference or to retrieve details quickly. At the very least, files should be sorted and arranged logically by topic or theme, using whatever colour coding or file dividers will help you. There is nothing more frustrating than a desperate search through files of messy, ill-kept notes for a vital quotation or date. Doing all this requires a bit of self-discipline: this is another aspect of the difference between university and school.

Referencing

The requirement to produce full references marks university work off very visibly from school work. It is easy to think that the lecturer who marks you down because you put the title of a journal article in *italics* instead of 'quotation marks' really ought to get out more. However, the reason for this insistence on correct referencing is that the historian has not only to show that the material is not made up but also to allow anyone who might wish to, to check it. Research students often start their work by following up the references in standard books or articles. And you must expect your lecturers to do it with your work on occasion. Sometimes the original source can be surprisingly different from the version quoted in the book or article; the writer David Irving lost his libel action against Penguin Books for labelling him a Holocaust denier because Penguin's main witness, Professor Richard Evans, had gathered a team of researchers together to check Irving's footnotes. Proper referencing is undoubtedly a chore but it is the courtesy the historian pays his or her readers, sources and subject; it is important to learn it from the start.

That said, there is no general consensus about the correct form of referencing in history. Many universities insist on the Harvard system, in universal use in the social sciences though seldom seen in history books. The Harvard system, which lists sources in a simple alphabetical list at the end and refers to them within the text by name and date – for example, (Lang, 2008) – is easy for the writer to use but can be obtrusive for the reader. Footnoting is easier on the eye. If you are given the choice, choose the convention you feel most at ease with; otherwise, follow the system you are told to use – to the letter.

Plagiarism

Plagiarism is not quite the same as simply copying. It means taking someone else's work and passing it off as your own. Universities take plagiarism very seriously; in extreme cases a student may even be expelled. However, you may not be entirely clear about what is so wrong with plagiarism. After all, we all have to get our information from somewhere. There is nothing wrong with quoting from someone else's work, even occasionally at length, but the quotation(s) should not be so long as effectively to constitute the main body of your work: imagine, for example, an essay on Dickens that consisted almost entirely of a chapter copied out from *Oliver Twist*. And they must be acknowledged and references provided. Not to do so is at best lazy and at worst deliberately fraudulent; indeed, at its very worst, where you are seeking financial gain from your writing, it is a criminal offence. Cutting and pasting material from the internet is an extremely unwise thing to do, not least because it can be unmasked by a simple Google search. There is no need to feel intimidated by these strictures: as long as you acknowledge your sources you cannot be accused of plagiarism. I deal in a bit more detail with using the internet in the next section.

Reading

It's not that long since an instruction to read had people reaching for books. Nowadays, students turn first to the internet. The advantages of having such a vast store of information sitting on your desktop are too obvious to require outlining here, but you may also find that some lecturers are hostile to excessive use of the internet. Some ban students from using popular sites such as Wikipedia and even the Google search engine. You may think that this is an extreme reaction. But many students use the internet badly, getting material from the first couple of sites that come up on a Google search and never cross-checking or even finding out where the information came from in the first place. If the internet is used in this unthinking, uncritical way, it can be almost as haphazard as asking for historical information from passers-by in the street.

Before reading anything – book, journal or website – ask yourself what you are reading *for*. Frequently, you will be looking for factual information: What actually happened? Who were these people? What, in short, is the story? Encyclopaedia internet sites can often be very good for this sort of task, though you should always be aware of their limitations: even quite major themes can be omitted. But you should also look at printed encyclopaedias, which usually sit unopened on library shelves but often carry far more information than their web versions. University libraries will also have biographical reference works, especially the excellent *Oxford Dictionary of National Biography*, which also exists online. Such reference materials do not usually need to be footnoted or referenced within your text, but they should be included in your bibliography; for websites, the home website address will usually be sufficient unless it is a particularly difficult page to find. The rule is: if you used it, include it.

Alongside fact-checking there are two other main types of reading to undertake: contemporary reading from the period you are exploring, and secondary works.

Contemporary works

Students do not do anything like as much of this type of reading as they could do, yet it is at once the most fruitful and the most enjoyable form of historical reading there is. An inspector's report on a workhouse tells you far more about attitudes towards the nineteenth-century poor than any secondary work can. I recently got a much better idea of popular attitudes in Britain towards appeasement from reading the letters people sent to the candidates in the first by-election after the Munich conference than I could ever have obtained from reading someone else's analysis. There is no substitute for going back to the sources, and you should do it as much as you can, whether or not it is a requirement of your course. Where you find your source material will depend on the subject, but this is where the internet can come into its own. Newspaper archives are easy to search and *The Times Online* is an excellent resource for almost any topic from the late eighteenth century onwards. Museums, galleries and archives are putting their holdings online for precisely this sort of use. Getting original material from the web is always impressive and will go a long way towards mollifying any lecturer smarting because you began by looking at Wikipedia.

Secondary works

This category covers anything written by historians. An historical work can be a secondary source on its subject matter but primary material for studying the time during which it was written. Your first encounter with university reading will usually come via a dauntingly extensive reading list handed out by a heartlessly enthusiastic lecturer and your reaction may well veer from disbelief to despair. However, remember that the secondary reading is principally to give you an idea of how historians have interpreted the period, so that if you already have an idea of the outline of events from your 'fact-checking' reading you will find it much easier to read the secondary works. (Try not to use secondary materials simply as sources of factual information. It suggests you have not actually spotted that they carry their own interpretations.)

Secondary materials come in three broad categories:

- articles
- popular books
- academic books.

Articles are relatively short pieces of detailed research on a particular issue, often fairly narrow in scope, and usually published in an academic journal. Helpfully, many articles carry a summary of their argument and have a separate conclusion. You should certainly read the whole article, but there is seldom much need for a first-year undergraduate to keep a note of more than its main conclusions.

Popular books are aimed at a general readership and usually wear their scholarship lightly, with few or no footnotes or references and sometimes no index. This seldom bothers the general reader, but does make it harder to check the evidential basis for the author's argument. None of this necessarily makes such books 'bad' history, but lecturers will expect you to be able to point out the shortcomings of the popular history approach.

Academic books are usually distinguished by a plethora of footnotes and a lack of illustrations. The quality of the writing can vary and some academic writing is, frankly, dull, but remember that life cannot be constantly entertaining and it is better for a writer to err on the side of dullness than on the side of inaccuracy (though many historians manage to write both interestingly and accurately). You may legitimately comment in a review or report that the book's style is dry or heavy, but do not offer 'boring' as your overall verdict on it – to do so is immature. More important is to draw out the book's argument or standpoint. Does the writer stress one factor over every other? (many historians do). Has the writer relied too much on one particular type of source? For example, it is common for historians to rely too heavily on official documents simply because these tend to be published and therefore easily accessible; would other types of source material be likely to change the historian's ideas? Above all, do you find this writer's argument convincing and can you say why?

Realistically, you will probably have to take some short cuts in your reading, using the index to home in on the most relevant sections. Some indexes are detailed enough to help you do this easily, while others offer nothing more than unhelpful lists of page numbers. Life is like that. The bibliography can indicate other titles to look at. Comparing the bibliographies in different books will often highlight the main texts you ought to consult. If you can summon the courage to do it, try reading a chapter, or at least a section of a chapter, *without taking any notes*; then reflect for a moment on what you have read and note down only what seem to have been the one or two main points the writer was trying to make. This takes a bit of courage, but it will help you read more in the time available to you and build up an idea of the overall shape of scholarship on your topic.

Finally, a quick word about *historiography*. This has been called the 'study of the study of history' and it involves studying historians in terms of both what they have written and the times in which they wrote it. Some teachers and lecturers approach it with great enthusiasm and, indeed, there is much to be learned about a society from the way it looks at its past. For example, no study of the Victorians would be complete without a look at their reverence for the Middle Ages and Victorian historians are obviously central to this. However, historiography can be an acquired taste; more importantly, it can get in the way of becoming familiar with the historical period itself.

Students sometimes wonder whether they should go into the historiography of every topic they study. It is not possible to give a blanket answer. If such a debate is both relevant and interesting then you should certainly include it, but this will not always be the case. In some periods the historiographical debate is so central that no one can really claim to have studied the subject to degree level without engaging at some level with it. The fierce arguments that rage between historians about Stalin's role in the purges is a clear example. Other topics and periods are less animated by historiographical controversy and it may not be so necessary to bring it into your work. If in doubt, you should ask your lecturer in good time; whatever happens, remember that history is ultimately about learning about the people of the past rather than the historians who have studied them.

Your studies or your life?

The experience of settling into university is about much more than your degree subject: as well as a seemingly endless round of social invitations you may find yourself having to deal for the first time with landlords, shopping bills, housemates, sports trials, music or drama auditions, insurance, cleaners, debating societies, chaplains, political canvassers and student societies covering everything from Esperanto to clog dancing. In the frenetic pace of student life it can be easy to lose sight of the demands of your studies and the strictness with which deadlines are enforced can come as a nasty shock. If you miss one without a very good reason you may well find that the lecturer refuses to mark your work. Check before submitting work by email that this is acceptable: not all lecturers relish having their ink and paper taken up by incoming student assignments. Such is the emphasis put upon the prompt submission of work that you may find that, instead of handing your work directly to your lecturer, you are required to hand it in to a central office from where the lecturer will collect it. These new procedures may take a bit of time to get used to but you must observe them: students who do not hand work in or continually miss deadlines are laying themselves open to sanctions.

Students usually find their own ways of balancing academic work and other commitments; the important thing is to find a space in your weekly schedule for work and to stick to it. Equally important, though, is to let the rest of your life at university inform and enrich your historical studies. One of the most fruitful aspects of student life can be the exchange of ideas with people studying very different disciplines and, history being the study of all human activity, all of these contacts can help you understand the past more fully. By the same token, your historical understanding should help you make a valuable contribution to debate and discussion on any number of topics.

The first year of any university course undoubtedly presents the student with a steep learning curve; properly handled, however, it can be a richly rewarding and horizon-widening introduction to the full range of what history has to offer.

2 Benchmarks

Mary Abbott

History surrounds us. The oldest structure above ground in Cambridge, where I live, is the endearingly clumsy tower of St Benet's Church, built getting on for a thousand years ago by masons who seem to have lacked confidence in their work. There are Roman bricks in the walls of St Peter's, north of the river, where the 'very minor' Roman settlement was – the church was built in the twelfth century and more or less rebuilt at the end of the eighteenth. In May 1903 the grave of a wealthy Iron Age man was discovered in a drainage trench on the western outskirts of the town. The grave goods it contained – bronze brooches, an arm ring and horse-ornaments – are in the collection of the Museum of Archaeology and Anthropology.

History, broadly interpreted, is a major source of leisure and pleasure. At the cinema, 'history' is big box office. Books about historical episodes and historical figures are best-sellers. Newspapers illustrate articles about today's events with potted histories of the topic. Exhibitions with historical themes draw crowds to museums and galleries. Historic towns are tourist magnets. Properties managed by the National Trust and English Heritage pull in visitors. People don't just consume history – they live it. Members of societies such as the Sealed Knot, which re-enacts the battles and sieges of the English Civil War, spend their spare time in 'the past'. Men and women with no academic training delve enthusiastically in archives to uncover the roots of their family trees.

How does this ambient history compare with the academic subject you will study as an apprentice historian? Some is, of course, utter garbage, but even a meticulously researched documentary film is likely to lack the scholarly hallmark of references, identifying sources and thus enabling viewers to examine the underpinning evidence for themselves.

In the UK, Subject Benchmarks, devised by groups with an interest in the well-being of university education, and published by the Quality Assurance Agency, serve as the gold standard for honours degrees. The design of degree courses and the performance of graduating students are measured against the benchmarks for their subject. And though these have been produced by and for universities in the UK, they are consistent with European university standards and with the expectations of universities in North America.

The History Benchmark Statement was compiled in 2000 by a team of 16 drawn from universities in England, Scotland and Wales, following consultations involving the wider academic community, including major Subject Associations such as the Economic History Society, the Historical Association and the Royal Historical Society. The benchmarks were reviewed in 2006 and amended to take account of changes in resources available to students as a result of the electronic revolution and to give a greater emphasis to the use of visual material and opportunities for fieldwork. The employability of history graduates was also underlined. You can find the History Benchmark Statement at www.qaa.ac.uk/academicinfrastructure/benchmark/statements/History07.asp.

You will be reassured to learn that, by the time they graduate, students at the 13 dental schools in the UK are expected to be able to demonstrate specific knowledge and understanding of, for example,

diseases and disorders of the oral cavity and associated structures, their causes and sequelae together with the principles
of their prevention, diagnosis and management.

The *Online Medical Dictionary* (http://cancerweb.ncl.ac.uk/cgi-
bin/omd?sequelae, accessed 21 December 2007) defines 'sequelae'
as 'a condition following as a consequence of disease'.

In contrast to the Dental Benchmark Statement, the one for
history does not prescribe the content of degree courses or, indeed,
methods of teaching and assessment – though it identifies the
essay as 'a central component'. Instead it defines the skills and
qualities of mind that a history degree should foster. Students
and their supporters will be comforted to learn that many of
these skills and qualities of mind are identical to those sought
by a wide range of employers.

Perhaps it is old-fashioned to ask a student what she is 'reading'
at university but, for history, the phrase still holds good. Full-
time university students commit themselves to the equivalent of
a full-time job – getting on for 40 hours a week when time spent
in lectures and seminars, in the library and working in Hall or
at home is added up. Take away time spent in classes, in fieldwork
of various kinds, in planning and writing assignments, and in
revising for and sitting exams and you will find that you have a
good many hours over. Most of them should be spent reading
either in the library or in a room of your own. This demands
self-discipline, self-direction and the ability to gather evidence
and analyse it – all generic employability skills acquired through
the study of history at university. Incidentally, university librarians
believe that historians will be the last group of academics left in
their libraries – digital texts cannot replace the physical evidence
provided by a manuscript or the original edition of a book or
journal.

'The past is a foreign country: they do things differently there',
as L.P. Hartley (1895–1972) put it in his novel *The Go-Between*,
published in 1953. Awareness of the 'otherness' of the past is
an essential quality of the historian's mind. Degree courses in

history train students for the role of sophisticated and sympathetic time-travellers, whether their journey takes them to Germany in the fifteenth century or China in the twentieth. The apprentice historian must learn to accept that a highly educated, highly intelligent man of the 1480s (there were few highly educated women in the 1400s) could accept the theory of witchcraft elaborated in *Malleus Maleficarum* (*The Hammer of the Witches*), published in 1486, and endorse the strategies its authors proposed for extorting confessions and punishing those found guilty. What was believed to be an 'attack from the invisible world' of witches led to the notorious trials at Salem, Massachusetts, in 1692.

Your course will also reflect the benchmark's insistence that it should cover a sufficiently long span of time to enable students to observe the patterns of continuity and change; that its geographical scope should embrace a range of societies and cultures. You will learn to 'read', evaluate and interpret texts, visual and material evidence produced in the period under scrutiny, and you will be introduced to a range of specialisms.

To give an example to illustrate these bald statements, let me outline the range of material that second-year history students encounter on a module exploring family and gender in England (the study of gender is an example of a specialism) between 1650 and 1850 (a period marked by continuities and change). Students analyse and discuss extracts from texts of the period (primary sources) including Sarah Scott's *Millennium Hall* (1762), a fantasy about a humane and harmonious community governed by wise single women, and *An Essay upon Nursing and the Management of Children from their Birth to Three Years of Age by William Cadogan of Bristol MD* (1748).

Dr Cadogan pointed the contrast between the healthy, ill-clad breastfed child of a poor family in the country and

the Heir and Hope of a rich Family [who] lies languishing under a Load of Finery, that overpowers his Limbs, abhorring and rejecting the Dainties he is crammed with, till he dies a Victim to the mistaken Care and Tenderness of his fond Mother.

Cadogan's *Essay* was addressed to a Governor of the Foundling Hospital, established in 1739 by Thomas Coram, a merchant who was horrified to see dead and dying babies abandoned in the streets of London. Students of Family and Gender undertake fieldwork in the Foundling Museum where, along with a range of visual and material primary sources, they see a reconstruction of the magnificently decorated Council Room, hung with the original paintings of the other London hospitals, where the Governors of the Foundling Hospital deliberated. They can examine the reproduction of a print of 1749 showing society women watching mothers taking part in the lottery for places in the hospital (demand outran supply by a ratio of three to one) and examples of the tokens mothers left with their babies in preparation for the day, which rarely came, when they were able to retrieve their children: a broken shell with 'James son of James Concannon gent, Late or Now of Jamaica' scratched onto it; a purse embroidered with the initial 'MD'; a commonplace mother-of-pearl gaming counter shaped like a fish; a coin cut in half. Historians have described objects as 'quite literally dumb' but, although their particular resonances are lost, these trifles cry out. Infants entering the Hospital were given new identities, a fresh start intended to distance them from their unfortunate origins in fornication and poverty. The Museum displays a list of the – sometimes fanciful – names bestowed on the 1,344 foundlings admitted between 1741 and 1756: Augustus Caesar, Geoffrey Chaucer, William Shakespeare, Admiral Benbow, Sweet Rose – names that remind me of those that plantation owners bestowed on their slaves.

As well as interrogating the pictures and artefacts on display, students are encouraged to evaluate the curators' interpretation of them. Elsewhere, students see paintings that illustrate the ways in which the wealthy chose to have their families portrayed.

The evidence that these students gather, evaluate and use to construct arguments in response to the questions posed by their teachers is, like the evidence available to the professional historians whose interpretations they draw on, incomplete. Eighteenth-century publications, whether they are works of fiction, such as

Millennium Hall, or manuals like Cadogan's, were produced by highly literate men and women for readers who had the money to acquire them and the leisure and skills to consume them. London foundlings benefited from Cadogan's advice on child-rearing; it is unlikely that any of the tradesmen who supplied the Foundling Hospital had access to a copy of his *Essay*.

All the second-year students who choose Family and Gender as one of their modules take a compulsory module on Europe, 1850–1900 in parallel. This offers the geographical scope missing from Family and Gender. To complete this module successfully, students have to demonstrate an understanding of the political geography of nineteenth-century Europe; make a critical assessment of nationalism in Germany, France, Russia and the Austro-Hungarian Empire; and analyse documents relating to such key concepts as nationalism, conservatism, liberalism, socialism, communism and Zionism.

Here again, scholars, and the students who depend on their endeavours to an even greater extent when dealing with events outside the English-speaking world, face issues of unsound evidence and conflicting interpretations.

Given the fragmentary and often contradictory nature of the evidence that has come down to us, it is possible for two historians of equal skill and integrity to come up with radically different interpretations of the same topic. In the course of three undergraduate years, history students are expected to achieve the intellectual independence and confidence to – in the words of the Benchmark Statement – 'gather, select, organise and synthesise large quantities of evidence', 'to formulate appropriate questions and to provide answers to them' and to articulate an argument 'in clear, lucid and coherent prose'. But, as the benchmark insists, it is the mark of a good historian to be open to persuasion and ready to change his mind when confronted with new evidence or a convincing counterargument.

3 Sources and resources

Mary Abbott

Sources

Sources: See 'Documents' – today, this definition taken from a book on the historian's craft published 30 years ago would be considered excessively narrow. Documents remain the historian's core source but most practitioners would now acknowledge the contribution that the spoken word, images and artefacts can and should make to our understanding of the past.

Historians traditionally divide their sources into two broad categories: primary and secondary. Primary evidence is, strictly speaking, first-hand. That does not mean that it is true. People close to events are often emotionally involved and they rarely see the whole picture. Try a simple test: station trustworthy people opposite each other and invite them to describe what they can see.

Uncertainty gives rise to reinterpretation and debate between historians. Historiography is the label we use for the history of writing about the past: debate is an important strand of historiography. Thus *The Debate on the French Revolution* is an apt title for the book Peter Davies published in 2006 to guide students through a forest of commentaries and approaches from Edmund Burke's *Reflections on the French Revolution*, published in 1790, through the publications prompted by the bicentennial of 1989 and beyond.

From our standpoint in the present, we know the end of many stories – we have the disadvantage of hindsight. Read diaries written in Britain in the summer of 1940 after the evacuation from Dunkirk and the Fall of France and it becomes evident that the Victory Parades of 1945 were by no means the expected outcome. Serious, scholarly, virtual or counterfactual history – the 'what if', 'just supposing' alternative narratives – are useful correctives to blinkering hindsight. Ian Kershaw's *Fateful Choices: Ten Decisions that Changed the World, 1940–1941* (2007) is a recent example of an exploration of uncertainty by a leading scholar in his field. The first of Kershaw's fateful choices, made on 28 May 1940, was the British government's decision to fight on.

The nature and volume of the historian's sources and the skills required to make effective use of them vary with the topic and the task upon which a scholar is engaged. The materials used by historians working on superficially similar topics may be strikingly different. If you set out to examine Horatio Nelson's role in the British victory at Trafalgar in 1805, you would concentrate your attention on the surviving logs and journals kept on board the vessels involved in the action. A medical casebook with Nelson as its subject would draw on accounts of his life and death, the many portraits of this 'fascinating little fellow' and medical and psychological literature from the eighteenth century to the present day. If, on the other hand, you were working on the national response to Nelson's death, you would explore a much wider range of materials, which might include state papers, the press, private letters and diaries, theatre posters, commemorative wares manufactured in precious metal, enamel, glass, pottery and textiles, and the campaigns to raise monuments – including a number of columns – to his memory. It may come as a surprise to discover that the column in Trafalgar Square was not erected until 1843.

Equally, the nature and volume of evidence and the skills required of an interpreter of the past depend on the stage that you have reached in your practice as an historian.

The acquisition of the full range of techniques and skills that enable an historian to

- understand
- assess
- put into context
- interpret

complex historical data is the business of the postgraduate.

In your first year as an undergraduate writing on the topic of accusations of witchcraft in seventeenth-century New England, you might use five or six chapters or articles recommended by your tutor. As your student career progresses and you develop the skills and independence expected of a history graduate, you will be required to read more widely and deeply, tackling monographs (specialised and authoritative book-length studies) and papers published in learned journals. Work on an undergraduate dissertation would almost certainly involve the use of primary sources – now happily available at http://etext.virginia.edu/salem/ witchcraft as a result of the University of Virginia's Documentary Archive and Transcription project on the Salem witch trials.

Universities and colleges expect students reading for a degree in history to demonstrate an ability to work on a broad canvas and in depth; to attempt to pose and address questions about big issues. But even when their focus is very narrow, few practitioners can hope to retrieve and verify every scrap of evidence on their topic. Historians are obliged to depend on the work of their predecessors. We must, however, strive to be constantly vigilant, critical clients rather than passive receivers.

It is a commonplace that the makers of our sources – the historical actors – were prisoners of their rank, gender and values. So, to a degree not always sufficiently acknowledged by students, are the professional historians of today.

A good historian is a sceptic who takes nothing at face value, who is ever open to new ideas and who is prepared to modify her views in the light of new evidence or persuasive argument. History is a forensic discipline – it's not surprising that a good proportion of history graduates go into the legal professions.

According to the task or, perhaps, the stage of the task on which you are engaged, you will approach your sources as detective, judge, juror or advocate. Indeed, you will frequently assume these mantles in turn. The order in which the roles are listed mirrors the process of data collection, evaluation and argument in which you engage when you undertake an assignment.

Whatever the nature of the historian's sources, the essential questions in their interrogation remain constant:

- Who made the source?
- When?
- Why?
- What accounts for its preservation?
- Is it genuine?
- Has it been tampered with?
- Is it corroborated by other pieces of evidence?
- How scrupulously has it been interpreted?

Resources

One of the key resources for a history student is the expertise of the librarians who manage the collections of college, faculty and university libraries. Make friends with the librarian with history in her portfolio.

Most libraries use the Dewey system of classification, which assigns the numbers between 900 and 999 to history – with interruptions for geography at 910 and biography at 920. In practice, history books are widely scattered so that works on the history of the family sit with other material on the family on the sociology shelves, while the history of trade unions sits with other material on trade unions in the economics section. In the course of your undergraduate career, you are likely to use books shelved in anthropology, geography, history, history of art, literature, politics, economics, sociology and science and technology.

Make a habit of consulting the multi-volume *Oxford English Dictionary* (*OED*), on paper or online, to confirm or modify your understanding of words in the context of the past. The *OED* is a museum of words. A sexual encounter might be described as 'naughty' in texts written three or four hundred years apart. In the sixteenth or seventeenth century naughtiness meant something 'morally bad or wicked'; in the noughties of the twenty-first century naughtiness is trivial. Today 'nondescript' means 'ordinary'. Two hundred years ago, as readers of Patrick O'Brian's novels will be aware, a 'nondescript' was an exotic plant or animal not yet described by naturalists.

As a student of English history, you will benefit from those great monuments to Victorian energy, the *Victoria County History* (*VCH*) and the *Dictionary of National Biography* (*DNB*). The old *DNB* has been superseded by the *Oxford Dictionary of National Biography*, most useful in its continuously updated, searchable online version.

You will find compendia of historical facts, such as the series published by Macmillan and written by Chris Cook and others, invaluable quick-reference aids. The volume covering the years 1760 to 1830 includes among its many helpful tables and lists the names of bishops and archbishops, members of governments, and the franchise in English boroughs before the Great Reform Act of 1832: in the borough of Cambridge the voters were its freemen; in Reading, householders who paid the poor rate; and in Northampton, the male householders not in receipt of poor relief – the 'pot wallopers', as they were known.

Atlases provide you with evidence of the physical geography that shaped life in the past. Historical atlases supply graphic commentaries on the histories of populations, economics, religious change and the causes and consequences of conflict. As with tables of statistics, maps tend to look to the naive eye like definitive statements of fact. They are, of course, the products of processes of selection and interpretation, to be used, like all the historian's resources, with sceptical care.

Take the History Benchmark's new emphasis on visual evidence on board. Enliven an assignment on a topic from the reign of George III or George IV with a discussion of the acid caricatures produced by James Gillray or his fellow satirists, or a paper on English politics in the 1930s or 1940s with work by the great cartoonist David Low.

Gillray represents George III not as 'mad' or 'wise' but, in the company of his wife, Queen Charlotte, as a monument of avarice. 'His Highness in Fitz' depicts the Prince of Wales making vigorous love with Mrs Fitzherbert, a Roman Catholic woman whom he regarded as his wife (a union outlawed by the Act of Settlement of 1701); they married in a clandestine ceremony (outlawed by Hardwicke's Act of 1753) and in defiance of the Royal Marriages Act of 1772, which required the King's consent.

Three of Low's cartoons, published in the *Evening Standard* in May and June 1940, illustrate the crisis Britain faced. 'All Behind You, Winston' appeared four days after Churchill took over as Prime Minister: the Labour leaders Attlee, Bevin, Morrison and the displaced Chamberlain march with him, sleeves rolled up and ready for action, at the head of a great army of men in civilian dress. 'To Fight Another Day', which came out on 8 June, celebrated the rescue of 338,226 survivors from the beaches of Dunkirk. 'Very Well, Alone' (18 June) echoed Churchill's speech proclaiming the forthcoming 'Battle of Britain', which he predicted would be the Empire's and Commonwealth's 'finest hour'.

4 Libraries – physical and virtual

Penny King

Y ou will all have used libraries in the past and may think
you know all there is to know about them. When you
walk into the university library for the first time, make
sure you don't fall into this trap.

Not all libraries are the same. I'm not just talking about the
physical layout or the classification scheme used to organise the
stock (although you will find that more and more universities
and colleges use the Dewey Decimal Classification scheme, which
is reassuring if you've used public or school libraries in the past)
– the services and support offered to students varies enormously.
It will pay dividends if you find out early on what help is available
to you and how to use it.

The physical library

Ask students what they expect libraries to provide and most will
say 'books'. But there will be a great deal more than that: journals,
newspapers, DVDs and videos (including pertinent off-air record-
ings), CDs, audio tapes, maps, statistics, annual reports, abstracts
and indexes, slides, photos, artefacts and specialist collections,
for example. Not to mention computers, wireless networks,
scanners and a variety of environments and resources for group
or individual study.

Whatever the library holds will be detailed in the catalogue, which these days is almost certainly a computer catalogue. This has a number of advantages as you can search it in a variety of ways – by author, title, subject and classification number. Some library catalogues will allow you to search for items specifically for your course or on your reading list, for journal titles or by ISBN. Increasingly library catalogues also include electronic resources such as e-books.

Librarians as a resource

Your library will almost certainly offer some form of induction for new students: a drop-in tour, an online induction through the library website or a scheduled and subject-specific session. Take advantage of the induction and find out exactly what the library can offer you as well as guidance on accessing the resources the library holds, both physical and digital.

Most academic libraries have subject-specialist librarians who have an intimate knowledge of your subject and of your course as well as the library's history-related stock. These are good people to identify and make friends with!

Subject librarians provide a range of services and activities including some, or all, of the following:

- An *appointment system* to help individual students with research skills. This is particularly useful when you are just starting an assignment or your dissertation – your subject librarian will be able to help with tips and pointers for your literature search.

- *Phone, email and other online enquiries* – especially useful if you are a distance learner and live or study some way from the main library.

- Production of history and other *guides* to the library collections.

- *Information skills training* on a whole host of subjects, from finding journal articles or using databases to referencing and tips for internet searching.

- Involvement in educational technology and *learning environments*; some, or all, of your course may be delivered through a VLE (virtual learning environment).

The virtual library

Your library will have a website – the best ones are a second library in themselves. They provide 24/7 access to a wide range of digital resources including e-books and journals, databases, online guides and other information. The stock of the virtual library can't be snapped up by the first reader to arrive and will be available to you both on and off campus.

Most of these digital resources are not free: the library has taken out a subscription to them. A general search on Google may take you to the home page of, say, *The Journal of Modern History*, but, to *read* the article you want, you will have to identify yourself as a student at an institution that subscribes to the journal. Search within the library website and you can avoid a frustrating time with dead-ends and requests for passwords or payment.

So what resources are you likely to find within the virtual library?

Databases

A database is a giant journal index covering hundreds or even thousands of journals. It makes good sense then to use these as your first port of call as you can trawl a large number of journals fairly speedily.

Databases generally fall into one of three categories:

- Those that include the full text of articles, such as *Academic OneFile* or *Blackwell Synergy*. But remember that these databases tend to cover quite a wide range of subjects, not just history, and do not include full text for all articles.

- Those that give an abstract of the article, but not the full text. As its name suggests, *Historical Abstracts* is the prime example here – a short paragraph gives an outline of the article but you need to go to the journal to read the article in its entirety.

- Those that merely give a citation, which will enable you to track down the article elsewhere. Such a database would be the *British Humanities Index*, which indexes over 320 humanities journals and magazines published in the UK and other English-speaking countries.

Databases do not necessarily cover the whole run of the journal. Typically databases go back no further than the 1970s. However, many are now extending their coverage backwards and some, such as *JSTOR*, include full text articles of journals from the 1930s or even earlier.

Journals

Armed with the information and reference you have found through your database search you can check whether your library subscribes to the journal you want. Unfortunately databases index many more journals than most libraries hold, but the key journals for history students will be in stock in either physical or digital format. Publishers increasingly produce online versions of journals and most university libraries hold hundreds in this format.

There may be a way to save your favourite journals and journal articles within the virtual library, which will save you time in the future and possibly a lot of printing.

Books

Publishers are increasingly publishing books in an electronic format. Check what your library offers in the way of e-books and how to access them. Some key resources are already available to the history student, among them the *Oxford Dictionary of National Biography*, which has 56,000 biographies of people who shaped the history of the British Isles and beyond, from the earliest times. You can search this by name or by theme and the articles often contain both portraits and references to further reading.

Newspapers

Your library's website will almost certainly provide access to the main British newspapers, typically from the mid-1990s onwards.

A fairly new resource is *19th Century British Libraries Newspapers*. This provides runs of 48 newspapers – a mixture of national and regional papers specially selected to best represent Britain at that time. *The Times Digital Archive (1785–1985)* enables you to search and view almost everything from the newspaper including advertisements, obituaries and reviews.

Portals, subject gateways and other online resources

Subject gateways have been developed to pull together recommended websites in a subject area. These gateways guide you to resources that are of academic rigour and accuracy.

Voice of the Shuttle (http://vos.ucsb.edu) is one of the oldest humanities resources on the web. History is represented, as are related subject areas such as Anthropology, Architecture, Art History, Gender Studies, Politics and Government. Every link has a brief annotation.

History On-Line (www.history.ac.uk/search) is a section of the website of the Institute of Historical Research (IHR). This provides information on books and articles, current and past UK research (theses) as well as evaluated links to history-related websites.

Intute (www.intute.ac.uk) also provides access to recommended web resources. It has a Virtual Training Suite, which gives an excellent online tutorial to help develop your skills in using the internet to find high-quality information and resources. You will find the tutorial for historians at www.vts.intute.ac.uk/he/tutorial/history.

Using other libraries

Your institution's library is by no means your sole resource. Your library will be able to advise you about arrangements that may exist to allow you to use other local academic libraries, and you may well be able to use other university libraries for reference purposes outside term time. Always check before turning up on the doorstep – and take your university ID with you.

If you are studying British history, collections such as the National Archives in Kew are open to you. A plethora of information and material from the National Archives is available online through its website at www.nationalarchives.gov.uk.

Local studies libraries, normally attached to public libraries, can be an invaluable source for the history student.

For European and world history, resources are obviously more limited, but again your subject librarians should be able to help you to identify any relevant collections.

Search techniques

Before beginning any assignment, dissertation or project, it is essential that you carry out a thorough search for all types of information relevant to your subject. Information may be printed, electronic or audiovisual but, whatever the format, the following points need to be kept in mind:

• *Information searching is time-consuming* – so start as early as possible.

- *Be systematic in your research* – in order to cover all sources available.

- *Keep a record of your references* – you will need full details to trace your resources and list in your bibliography at a later date.

- *Keep a record of a successful search strategy* – it will save you working it out again when you want to update your research!

Defining the subject

Before you begin, you need to decide exactly what it is you are looking for:

- Clarify the meaning of your topic and/or particular words.

- Ask yourself questions about the subject – how can you break it down?

- Define your scope:

  - *Publication date* – how current does the information need to be?

  - *Range* – what type of document do you want to include (e.g. journal article/book review)?

  - *Language* – does it have to be in English?

  - *Geographical limits* – do you want to limit your search to material relating to a particular country or area?

  - *Country of publication* – do you think that this is going to prove important?

  - *Other limitations* – e.g. do you need to define the age or gender of the subject?

- What aspects of the subject do you want to include – broader or narrower? For a large topic should you choose a specific aspect?

Identifying keywords

Decide on your keywords or phrases that sum up the information that you want. Be as specific as possible.
  Think about:

- synonyms and related terms (resistance/revolt; Great War/ First World War);

- American terms and spellings (labour/labor; colour/color);

- plurals (lady/ladies; church/churches);

- acronyms and abbreviations (WW2/World War 2; UK/United Kingdom);

- changes in terminology when looking for older materials (consumption/tuberculosis; Common Market/European Community);

- the use of hyphenation (eighteenth-century/eighteenth century; timetable/time-table).

  Look in encyclopaedias and subject dictionaries to give you ideas for keywords. Your results will illustrate the importance of keyword selection.

Reviewing your search

Review the results from your initial search to decide whether your keywords have given you enough results/relevant results. If not:

- think back to your search terms and concepts and add or remove as necessary;

- use the help pages, online help or guide for the index or database you are using.

Combining keywords using Boolean operators

Boolean operators, or connectors, allow you to specify how you would like an electronic database to interpret your search by combining two or more words in a single search:

*   **AND** for words that join together two or more different concepts and narrow the search (children **AND** education).
*   **OR** for words that are similar in meaning, and to widen the search to include synonyms, abbreviations or variants in spellings (bubonic plague **OR** black death).
*   **NOT** to exclude keywords that are of no interest (exploration **NOT** Columbus). Be careful – **NOT** can also exclude relevant records (an article on Christopher Columbus may also mention exploration in general).
*   A combination can also be used (Cromwell **AND** Levellers **OR** Diggers).

Truncation

Using an electronic database, it is also usually possible to truncate words (use a root word and find all the words that begin with the letters you specify). Truncation symbols are normally * or ?. For example:

*   environ* would find environment, environmental, environ-mentalist;
*   polic* would find police, policeman, policewomen, policing;
*   behavio* would find behaviour, behavior, behavioural, behavioral.

Be careful – you could also get results that are not applicable or not relevant:

*   hero* would find heroic, hero, but also heroin.

Wildcards

Wildcards help you to search for variable characters or spellings *within* a keyword. Wildcard symbols could be ? or $. For example:

- organi?ation would find organisation and organization;
- defen?e would find defence and defense;
- wom?n would find woman and women.

Always use the online help for the databases you use – they don't always have the same features.

Identifying the appropriate research resources to use

The table on pages 40–43 summarises various research resources, their characteristics and how to make the best use of them.

Referencing

Whatever resources you use it is vital that you keep a full and accurate record. When you submit your work you will need to include a bibliography listing the sources that you have used.

There are a number of reasons for this: first, it is good academic practice and will demonstrate that your work is a serious piece of academic writing; second, it will tell your tutor how widely you have researched the topic; and, third, and perhaps most importantly, it is a guard against any question of plagiarism.

You will need to reference all the sources on which you relied. There are a number of recognised systems of referencing and you will need to check which is the system used by your institution. All the systems are similar in that they set out exactly how to cite the elements that go to make up a reference, for example:

Cook, C., 1998. *A dictionary of historical terms*. 3rd edn. Basingstoke: Macmillan Press.

Boardman, E., 2007. Catherine the Great's trip to the Crimea. *Heritage Review*, 37(1), pp. 29–33.

A guide to the referencing system used for your course will be available to you and it is important that you have a copy before you start writing your bibliography.

Resource	Characteristics	How to use it
Books	Can give a good overview, background information or access to in-depth research. An academic publisher will usually ensure that information is generally reliable and well researched.	• Use your library catalogue to find books held in the library. Think carefully about your keywords and use others if your search gives few or no results. • Use other libraries' catalogues to find out what other books have been published. For example, the British Library, public libraries, etc. COPAC (http://copac.ac.uk) gives free access to the merged online catalogues of the major academic and national libraries in the UK and Ireland. • Bibliographies (lists of materials on a particular topic) or online book services (e.g. Amazon) can also help you trace books.
Journals	Up-to-date: published quickly and frequently. Many are refereed. May contain information not published elsewhere.	• Use any subject guides available in your library to identify relevant printed journals available or use the 'journals' search on the library catalogue if one is available. • Check what electronic journals the library subscribes to on its website.

Resource	Characteristics	How to use it
Databases	Economical way to survey the literature of a particular subject area; generally quick and easy to use. Most databases provide references and abstracts (summaries) of articles and some may provide the whole article (full text).	• Use any subject guides available to identify relevant abstracts, indexes or databases to which your library subscribes. • Some databases cover all subjects, e.g. Academic OneFile (a database of many full-text journal articles covering all subject areas); and BHI (British Humanities Index – a database covering humanities, arts, politics, society). • Others are more specialised, e.g. Historical Abstracts for history, Sociological Abstracts for sociology, etc.
Newspapers	Good for current affairs and features on social topics and commentary on news as it happened. May contain useful book reviews.	• If your library subscribes to UK Newspapers online it is a good source to use as it searches concurrently archives of *The Guardian, The Times, Financial Times, The Independent* and *The Daily Telegraph* and their Sunday equivalents. • For older newspapers check what is available to you within your institution – or for local papers use local studies collections in public libraries.

Resource	Characteristics	How to use it
Videotapes and DVDs	Audiovisual material can provide an alternative perspective to printed material.	• Many libraries hold recordings of selected television programmes and may also have a collection of feature films. There are many excellent history programmes that have been televised and you should not ignore them as a source. • Feature films may also be of interest, but be careful – historical accuracy is often ignored for the sake of a good story!
Statistics and population trends	Useful to back up your argument if you can find figures to support your claims.	• Your library will hold a variety of statistical sources and it will pay to become familiar with what these are. • There are also some excellent free online sources of statistics, for example Great Britain Historical Database Online (http://hds.essex.ac.uk/gbh.asp) – a large database of British nineteenth- and twentieth-century statistics; or Histpop (www.histpop.org), which provides online access to the complete British population reports for Britain and Ireland from 1801 to 1937.

Resource	Characteristics	How to use it
Internet	Vast amounts of information, but is it reliable, good-quality, academic information?	• For academic information try academic websites before doing a general web search. The best place to start is a subject gateway, where you will find a collection of quality websites on a subject, e.g. Best of History Websites (http://besthistorysites.net) or Voice of the Shuttle (http://vos.ucsb.edu/) – a general subject gateway for Humanities research. • There is also a wide range of search engines that allow you to search for information on the internet, of which Google is probably the best known. Keep your search as precise as possible otherwise you will retrieve thousands of hits. Search engines are particularly useful for finding company or organisation information.
Other sources	Your librarians!	• Helpful as it may be to read items like this, nothing can substitute for talking to the subject librarians in your own library and finding out exactly what is on offer to you in terms of services, advice, guidance and research skills training.
	Other libraries	• Explore what other libraries you can access and find out if there are any that have specialised collections in your research topic that may be available to you.

5 Making notes

Mary Abbott

This chapter examines

- reasons for making notes
- the characteristics of effective notes
- strategies for note-making
- formats.

The characteristics of effective notes are described under the heading 'Essentials'. You have more options when it comes to strategies and formats.

Why make notes?

Notes are aids to

- concentration
- comprehension
- memory

and enable you to

- express, organise and control information and ideas.

Good note-making skills will help you to become an effective reader, listener and participant in discussion. Like many of the skills you should acquire as an undergraduate historian, the ability to make effective notes is transferable to the rough old world of paid employment.

Essentials

Notes must be

- accurate
- easy to trace back to their source
- in your own words
- organised
- useful.

Notes must be accurate because they are among the key components from which you construct

- written and oral assignments
- exam answers
- dissertations and other major projects.

Take particular care with

- proper names
- unfamiliar and technical vocabulary.

Sloppiness will undermine your tutors' confidence in your work and distract them from its merits.

Notes must be easy to track back to their source because references, wherever they appear, enable your readers to verify the evidence you have marshalled in support of your argument.

For printed material, always record the

- author
- title of the book, article and journal
- place and date of publication
- pages

on which your notes are based.

For digital sources always record the

- URL

and the date when you visited the site.

If you make notes on pictures or artefacts, whether in the permanent collections of museums or galleries or in temporary exhibitions, the label or catalogue entry should give you the necessary information. If your subject is a building, record its location and, if in the care of a trust or society, identify its custodian.

Get into the habit of using the system of referencing that your institution uses.

Notes must be in your own words. This

- protects you from the vice of plagiarism, which universities punish severely;
- enables you to test your understanding of the material you are working on. Until you can express an argument, idea or theory in your own words, you can't be confident that you have grasped it. Rephrasing helps you to understand and assimilate material.

Notes must be organised effectively. It is a waste of time to record information and ideas unless you can retrieve them.

Notes must be useful because, unless they are fit for the purpose for which you have made them, you will have spent your time in vain. Just as a skilled minute-taker omits irrelevant discussion, so the skilled student produces notes geared to the task in hand. Select and connect must be your watchwords.

Because you are selecting, notes should normally be significantly shorter than the text on which they are based. There are exceptions – passages of particularly dense argument that may require a lot of unpacking. If you decide to extract a long quotation or a complicated table, save time and avoid errors by photocopying. Be sure to acknowledge the source in the appropriate form.

Options

This section focuses on strategies and formats for note-making.

Strategies

Note-making strategies vary according to circumstances and from student to student.

Text is probably the easiest material to handle because you can set your own pace and work within your own span of concentration. You are more likely to get the gist of an argument if you read it straight through without pausing to make full notes. Keep a note of the pages that look particularly promising and provide yourself with a prompt to remind you of the reason for revisiting them. Well-chosen prompts will also help you to organise your notes.

Lectures are trickier. Handouts, old-fashioned transparencies or PowerPoint presentations will help you to identify the key points. Vocal emphases and gestures are other important clues. But the challenge of listening and understanding one point while noting an earlier one remains. It helps to do some homework: read the prescribed material. In the absence of set reading, use your initiative in the library or online. Try to set aside a few moments before the start of the lecture to tune into the topic.

Lean lecture notes are generally the best. In an ideal world you would set aside time to flesh them out after the lecture. But it takes courage to put your pen down and listen while other students are scribbling away. Collaborate with a friend, taking turns to listen with concentration until you have got the balance between listening and noting right.

Class discussions are even more of a challenge. The less structured the discussion, the harder it is for the note-taker. The bonus is that you have a chance, during or after class, to ask contributors to clarify, elaborate and supply references. But remember that the main purpose of the class is an exchange of ideas. Your pen should be idle more often than it is in motion.

Formats

These are very much a matter of choice, temperament and technology.

To illustrate the principle underlying note-taking, and indicate how the options for storage and retrieval of information have increased in the past century, let me quote from Reginald Lane Poole's obituary of Lord Acton, which was published in the *English Historical Review* of October 1902:

> He has been credited with a marvellous memory and this certainly came out conspicuously in his conversation. But his power of citing the appropriate text was artificially assisted by the habit which he early formed of making extracts of whatever struck him in his reading. These selections, made on slips of paper of a uniform size were arranged and classified and stored in a prodigious series of boxes and drawers. Of the advantages of such a method it is unnecessary to insist, and many laborious students may well envy the ease and security with which Lord Acton compressed the cream of his reading into compartments and was able to produce it at demand.

When you make notes, experiment, paying due regard to the essentials:

- accuracy
- traceability
- organisation
- relevance

and, of course,

- using your own words and acknowledging quotations.

Think about the ways in which you can draw attention to what you consider most important or connect related points. Underlining, or using block capitals, highlighters and arrows can be helpful. Mind maps or spray diagrams can be useful. But don't let presentation distract you from the substance of your notes. Reread them to make sure they make sense.

6 Classes – preparation and participation

Susan O'Brien

As a history student you will find your timetable made up of lectures and classes, no matter what modules or courses you take. The classes are usually labelled 'seminar', although they may also be called tutorial or workshop or 'small group work'. New staff and new students soon learn that a range of pleasures (or tortures – depending on your experience) take place under the umbrella heading 'seminar'. Even the group size of this small-group activity varies from university to university and from course to course – anything between 8 and 25 students being described in the same way. Although the group's size has an impact on the way the seminar works, there is no need there – or at any time – to become distracted by definitions or labels. It's much more important to understand what purposes your department, course or tutor intends for the sessions. Then you will be in a position to make the most of them.

Despite the variety of labels and activities, what distinguishes the class or seminar is its focus on *student participation*. Classes exist to enable you to engage in discussion with the tutor and, crucially, with one another. Your teachers, even those who gain great personal satisfaction from lecturing and believe it to be a valuable method of teaching, would agree that the seminar has much greater potential for you. Such potential is by no means always realised for reasons that will be analysed, explicitly and implicitly, in this chapter.

The purpose of this chapter is to enable you to get the most out of this form of teaching and learning. Looked at in purely economic terms, it is the most expensive form of learning you will undertake – more costly than lectures or individual study time spent in the library or elsewhere. Looked at another way, if you raise your own standards and effectiveness in a seminar you will inevitably lift the seminar for everyone else because *effective seminars depend on collaboration rather than the individual*. This is what in the language of politics and business is called 'win-win' and you don't have to be a goody two-shoes to achieve it. Much more to the point is to be *purposeful* and *instrumental*.

Seminar activities

All of the following can take place under the heading of class or seminar. Please note that my list is indicative, not exclusive:

- a presentation by one student followed by a discussion;
- short presentations by several students;
- a group presentation;
- a discussion, in which everyone is expected to participate, of particular questions and themes known in advance;
- working in pairs or small sub-groups on particular questions, followed by a whole-group session to share and focus on conclusions;
- working together to understand and interpret documents, statistics, maps or other materials;
- a debate, the group divided into two to defend or oppose a proposition;
- the pursuit of questions in a less structured format.

Why seminars?

I want to take some time over this because students, perhaps history students in particular, often regard classes or seminars as less vital than lectures. Or, more accurately, it takes them longer to learn the value of seminars. Lectures give you 'the stuff' to take away and, you hope, prepare for examinations and other assessments. What do seminars or tutorials 'give' you?

Students often say how much they would have benefited from more explanation about what tutors hoped for and expected from class sessions. They wish, with the benefit of hindsight, that someone had made explicit 'the rules of the game' and the thinking behind them. Tutors often think that they have done so, but have a tendency to underestimate the need both to take time over this at the beginning of the programme – and to come back to it periodically. On the other hand, there is a movement in higher education towards making these 'rules' much clearer to students. You can see this more clearly when you look at the changes to assessment. Many tutors now state in writing the criteria for assessment, informing students about what is expected. Not all academics will agree that it always helps to be explicit, but it is difficult to see why you should take several terms or semesters to stumble into understanding (and possibly never fully achieve it) when you can be told from the outset why historians (and others) so value the seminar.

The seminar has the potential to be:

* flexible;
* responsive – or at least more responsive to *your* interests and thinking about a subject;
* active;
* an exchange of ideas, knowledge or perspective.

We learn constantly through the exchange of ideas, knowledge and values in conversation. Whether we are talking about the latest film, a sports fixture or an item of current news, we are finding out about the subject of the conversation, ourselves and other people. What takes place in a seminar is a 'conversation' of sorts, but one that is formal, structured, artificial and controlled. Even though it doesn't precisely mirror any setting you will meet in other walks of life, it can help you enormously with many of the situations you are likely to encounter. Why is this and how can it help?

It does so because of the *values* intrinsic to the 'class' approach to learning and because of the *skills* it enables you to develop and practise. Many contemporary study guidebooks will emphasise the skills aspects of this learning, but we would still miss something essential to our study of the humanities if we overlook or ignore the values.

Looking at the *skills* first, a class or seminar enables you to develop and practise a good array. Make your own list before looking at the following:

- attentive and purposeful listening;
- intelligent questioning;
- formally presenting material or an argument 'live' rather than simply in writing;
- developing your argument and defending it;
- thinking 'on your feet';
- critically appraising the argument and evidence put forward by yourself and others;
- experiencing group dynamics and improving your under-standing of them;
- playing a range of roles within a group: leadership, supporting, challenging, ice-breaking, etc.
- problem-solving in a group.

Not all types of class allow you to develop a particular skill to the same extent, but across the range of your courses you will have plenty of opportunity to develop in all the areas listed above.

What about the *values* I claimed underlie the very existence of this approach to learning? Think about this for a moment and jot down your own list. My list comprises:

* tolerance and respect for the views of others: in this structured environment it is not in the 'rules of the game' to interrupt, shout, fall asleep, chat to your neighbour or walk out;

* open-mindedness and fairness: as part of the 'rules of the game' we have to weigh up all views expressed, make a critical judgement, and be prepared to have our own ideas challenged;

* recognition that there is often more than one perspective or interpretation: human experience is multidimensional, not readily reduced to formulae; we might wish there was a single, simple answer but have to recognise that human experience is more complex.

We need to add to this list (and your own) the fact that seminars also allow us to explore values through discussion – who thinks this and why? I hope you can see more easily why this form of learning can play a more important part in our development as historians and, more importantly, as intellectual and moral beings.

Now compare what you and I have said about the purposes and processes of 'classes' with the statement made by the former Chairman of Shell:

We are not looking for knowledge in our recruits. We are looking for mastery of the processes by which knowledge can be acquired and a maturity and sympathy gained from exposure to the mainstream of intellectual thought.

The document from which this passage was taken also asserted that:

The most important function of higher education is to inspire its students with a passionate inquisitiveness to continue learning through life. The humanities have a central role in redefining and transmitting a common culture of objectivity, tolerance, judgement by relevant evidence and fairness . . . Even within a single discipline, the humanities strongly emphasise the capacity to see a thing from several perspectives at once. 'It is the mark of a genius', F. Scott Fitzgerald wrote, 'to be able to hold two contradictory ideas in the mind at the same time.' In a world of abundant ambiguities and uncertainties, this is a valuable business attribute too . . .

Recruiters from companies in all sectors tell us that one of the principal qualities they seek is the ability to work well in a team. Many management development programmes feature multi-disciplinary teamwork and the capacity to motivate others often figures prominently in criteria for promotion.

Employers of humanities graduates agree that interpreting demanding texts, distinguishing fact from assertion, and appraising doubtful arguments offer a training in critical power and lucid expression . . . Business particularly values among its managers those who can stand back from the pressure of immediate opinions and alluring trends. Persuasive skills have their place but so does the ability to see through them.

Values and skills are so closely connected in this document that it is not particularly fruitful to try and separate them out. Instead, it is worth noting that the attributes desired by those who wish to be well educated in the humanities sense are also desired in business and industry (and, one might add, anywhere – including at home). And even a cursory analysis serves to inform us that these attributes must be developed and honed in dialogue and working with others.

All very fine but, you might legitimately ask, does it help me with the short-term and pressing goal of *passing assessments*? If asked to say which will most help you to answer the questions in examinations and assessments – lectures or classes – your tutors will say that seminars win every time. In seminars you are rehearsing the very processes that go into answering questions and solving problems: framing the possible responses, weighing the evidence, considering alternative interpretations and coming to conclusions.

The better your *preparation* and *participation*, the greater your chance of realising the potential of the seminar.

Preparation

The challenge of talking about history

I want to begin by acknowledging some of the challenges of history seminars. If the overall aspiration of the group is, to borrow Rostow's famous analysis of industrialisation, to 'take off into self-sustained growth', there are good reasons why some history seminars stay grounded. Leaving aside the possible explanation of poor teaching, part of the explanation lies in poor student preparation, and part in the intrinsic challenges of talking about history. Let's look at the latter first.

Getting a good exchange or discussion going in history is certainly challenging. There are particular difficulties not experienced to the same extent in other academic subjects. I don't offer this as an excuse, but make it as an observation from experience, starting with my own and adding to it that of hundreds of other Combined Honours history students who have been in a position to make informed comparisons between their subjects. In literature, philosophy and theology there is often a text to analyse together or a significant theoretical approach to work over. In human geography many classes have a practical and problem-solving dimension, again working from materials together. Sociology, women's studies, communication and media studies draw to some degree on contemporary society and culture, enabling students to make use of observation and experience as well as reading. Art history focuses on analysis of the visual and looking together can help group discussion.

Historians can – and do – make use of images, maps, documents, artefacts and newspaper clippings. They employ information technology. But, as history students know, these do not constitute the heart of the matter in most of their courses. Observation can be relevant (for example, observation of buildings and landscape) but it rarely is. Informed speculation or deduction can only play a limited part. Nor is personal experience of much help when you are studying the responses of backwoods farmers in the American Revolution, the nature of the family economy in fifteenth-century France or the operation of British imperial policy in nineteenth-century West Africa. Indeed, backwards projection of our own contemporary attitudes is positively unhelpful. The women and men of the fifteenth century are emphatically *not* ourselves dressed up in period costume, so we can't simply deduce how they would have responded or what they would have experienced.

The upshot of all this is that, as a student of history, you can feel underwhelmed by how little you can bring to the discussion and overwhelmed by your own lack of hard knowledge of events or phenomena, and by the array of interpretations.

Moreover, the speed at which you move through historical periods can add to your discomfort. My own first-year course in American history travelled from 1609 to 1968, leaving me with a residual feeling of anxiety throughout the seminars. Did I know who was president during the Civil War, let alone at any other time? What if anyone put me on the spot and actually asked me? Frozen and fearful, I endured the seminars never believing that I *knew enough* to make much contribution.

What can be done to face these very real challenges and to liberate yourself from those that merely cause unnecessary anxiety? What should *I* have done to increase my learning and my enjoyment?

I could start by simply recognising what the built-in challenges are and accept that it is not just me. The tutor knows this too. Next I can remind myself that I don't *have* to come to each session as a one-woman band, but can be part of a group who will tackle the questions together. Then I could try taking as much control as possible of the situation as an aid to building confidence and increasing my preparation and the time I spend on reading and thinking about the task. After all, I would not go on holiday without planning the itinerary, and taking a good hard look at the possibilities and what I wanted to get out of it. (OK, so I admit it – I might just take a package holiday and lie in the sun. But you take the point, I trust.)

TAKE CONTROL – LOOK AHEAD

- If the module has published aims or learning outcomes, spend time familiarising yourself with them – the assessment will be closely linked to them.

- Pay particular attention to the nature of the assessment and the nature and content of the classes or seminars.

- Work out what is being expected and what you hope to get from the course. Remember the holiday analogy: if you are on a rapid tour of European cities you expect to get a glimpse of each; Rome in a day is not the same as Rome for a week, although both are likely to include St Peter's and the Trevi fountain.

- Check out the library for resource strengths and weaknesses; possibly work out which assignment interests you most.

TAKING CONTROL – PRACTICAL PLANNING

- Convert all your modules into diary form, marking in lecture titles, seminar topics and seminar preparation periods.

- If you are responsible for a session (e.g. a presentation or chairing), mark this in and mark in additional preparation time.

- Plan your use of books and articles for the assignment by reserving them, copying articles or reading or note-taking ahead.

Even if you have been unable to keep to these plans, you will have a framework within which to deviate and tack about, according to need and reality. The first two weeks of a new course can often be slow, while the last two weeks are frenetic. You can even this out to some extent by anticipation and planning.

Participation

What I have to say about this is strongly influenced by my belief that learning in classes is not a competitive but a collaborative endeavour. It's not about getting 'one up' in some pecking order, but about learning. History tutors don't usually spend much time on the group-dynamic angle of the seminar and you won't be assessed on it. Nonetheless, the dynamic will play a significant part in your experience.

Being a member of the group

- The tutor does have control, but you are an adult participant.
- Make an effort to know and use the names of fellow students (your tutor should supply a list if you ask that everyone should have one).
- Think about the group dynamics as the weeks go on.
- Rearrange the furniture if necessary – it can make or mar a discussion.
- Let the tutor know of any problems – you both have a great deal to gain.

Students new to seminars often worry about *shyness* and *taking notes*.

SHYNESS
It may be that several weeks have gone by and you haven't felt able to make any contribution even though you have been well prepared. Many tutors periodically build into classes chances for

small groups of three or four to discuss a topic and this is often a real help in building confidence. But what can you do if this isn't the format and you wish you could join in? One possibility is to see the tutor outside the seminar and just explain that you find it difficult. Your tutor will probably ask if there is any approach that would help you (e.g. making an opening for you to ask a question, asking you directly, getting people to work in pairs and report back, or ignoring you until you feel ready). If you can manage it, you'll find it very helpful to take this approach. Otherwise talk to the person who runs your course or to a study skills adviser.

Try writing down a question before each class and look for an opportunity to ask it. A prepared question has the merit of being written down and gives you the chance to simply practise saying something.

Always remember that you are likely to overestimate everyone else and underestimate yourself. What's more, you are likely to overestimate what the tutor is expecting. Believe me when I say that tutors are aware when someone speaks for the first time and will be wanting to encourage you.

TAKING NOTES IN SEMINARS

Note-taking should not be your main activity in a seminar, but many people spend a lot of time doing it. Everyone wants to make the most of any good points that are made. But people also often hide behind note-taking, or do it compulsively. This is the time for thinking and engaging in discussion – just make enough notes to jog your memory. The basic posture in a seminar is to have your pen on the table and not in your hand. Limit yourself to headings, or a diagram approach. The main structure of the discussion and the major points are all that you need to take down. This is definitely not the occasion for capturing factual information. If you are worried about not having notes, ask your tutor for five minutes before the seminar ends when he or she can bring it to a conclusion and draw out the main points that have been made so that everyone can take notes.

Let's pick up again on the skills you will be using in the seminar and prepare for specific aspects of seminar participation.

Purposeful listening

Listening is greatly undervalued as a skill, possibly because it appears to be passive. But attentive and purposeful listening is an *activity*. Listening in this way requires interest, concentration, and the ability to put aside one's own preoccupations for the moment and be open-minded. Interestingly, comprehension and engagement are not determined by the fluency of the speaker. In fact, the fluency of the tutor can sometimes be a positive hindrance as he or she flows on, enthused by his or her own ideas. The more hesitant contributions of other students can often be more useful for you to use as a measure of your own comprehension. The basic rule is to listen as you would wish to be listened to: with respect and an imaginative sympathy.

Good listening is linked to astute question-asking and to useful interventions.

Question-asking – asking questions of the tutor or of one another

Questions *can* be asked during and after lectures. But we all know the blocks involved here. Questions in seminars can be for straightforward checking of your understanding ('Have I got this right?') or for pushing your understanding further ('If Countryman says . . . about the origins of the American Revolution, then how can Fleigelman have argued . . .?'). The role of curiosity is a vital one in the development of historical understanding – but also of understanding more generally. It is also one of the main ways human beings have of showing an interest – in a topic and in one another.

Asking questions may seem very straightforward but, as you know, it simply does not come easily. Many tutors invite you to take up questions from the most recent lecture or from readings.

The response is often a dead silence until one member dutifully dredges up a question, largely, one suspects, to rescue the poor tutor. Question-asking can be greatly improved by preparation and anticipation. You *know* this opportunity will come up and that it is valuable. Look at why you don't make more use of it. Is it poor organisation? (Where is that question you scribbled down in the lecture? Or was it as you were reading?) Or fear of appearing too ingratiating? Or lack of confidence and a fear that the question will be seen as revealing the stupidity of which you suspect yourself, but no one else?

POOR ORGANISATION

There are many ways to improve your organisation. Use bright stick-it labels in your file; write questions in coloured felt-tip; or have a coloured sheet at the back of your file and jot questions down as they occur.

FEAR OF APPEARING INGRATIATING

So, if you keep asking questions, might your fellow students and tutor perhaps think you are overdoing it? If this is likely, then it is a matter of disciplining yourself and learning to read other people's body language. This is a useful skill to have anyway.

FEAR OF APPEARING STUPID

This is the most common fear and the least likely to be realised. Almost everyone feels the same and the tutor knows it. Remember that the seemingly most obvious questions are not. Remember also that the tutor will be able to use any question to good advantage for the class, building on it. And remember that most tutors are so glad that you've asked and given them an opener that, even if the question could have been better expressed, they will be able to work with it. Abandon this fear as soon as you can, in true 'Blue Peter' fashion – use one you have prepared earlier. Get used to hearing your own voice out there and then keep practising.

Responding to the tutor's questions

Just as your questions can have different important purposes, so can those of the tutor. She may be checking up to see whether you have understood or she may be pushing on your thinking and opening up a new line of discussion and analysis.

Responding to questions is more familiar than asking. It is something that we all have had to do in school and we don't have to take the initiative, which makes it easier. But our responses can often be stunted. It takes practice to develop an answer that can lead the session forward. Perhaps your response can end with a further question, or invite others to comment. Don't worry about this. It really is a matter of practice and having patience with yourself.

Making a presentation

One of the most common of formats for the seminar is the student presentation. If you dread the idea of it you will almost certainly share this feeling with almost everyone else in the group. Even people who talk readily at home or in a group of friends can become tongue-tied when put into the more formal setting of a seminar (or a job interview, or a presentation at work, or chairing a meeting). These occasions require each of us to 'perform' or to take on a role, and the skills can be learned. Presenting a seminar will help you with all these formal performances.

Before you start to read and make notes, spend a little time thinking about the overall purpose of the presentation and your overall approach. Make a list of the features of a good seminar, from your experiences as a listener. It might include the following:

- it keeps to the time limit;
- it has a pace that allows easy listening;
- it provides an overview of the topic first – it does not go straight into detail;

- it uses quite short sentences and gives signals such as 'my first point';
- it gives a handout that summarises main points;
- it uses visual material;
- it raises questions for the group to discuss;
- it informs you of the sources used.

Notice that all these features show a high level of awareness about the listener – and less concern for detail and high level of content. A seminar is not a mini-lecture but a chance for discussion of big ideas or main arguments. If you provide too much detail, these aspects may be lost. So, take courage. It's not a waste of time to think about effective communication as well as content.

Assume, for example, that you have been asked to give a presentation of ten minutes' duration in your first-term module on Industrialisation in Britain, 1740–1830. The topic is the Consumer Revolution, 1740–80.

You know that the purpose of the presentation is to provide the basis for discussion – a kick-start for the remainder of the session. You don't need to provide all the material, only a number of pointers for discussion and some conclusions of your own to provoke interest.

The reading list is pretty long and you don't know which books or articles are best. Start with your course textbook, which has a good summary of about ten pages. It shows you that there is a debate among historians about whether a consumer revolution took place and, if so, when it started. *Here is one of the points for discussion.* Historians also argue about who the consumers were – who could afford the goods and where did they live?. *Perhaps this might make a second area for discussion,* although at this stage you're not sure how different it is from the first. Several of the writers mentioned in the textbook's bibliography are on your reading list. One of the works you consult has excellent illustrations and you decide to photocopy a few to pass round. *Here is a third dimension for the presentation.* By now you see how easy it would be to get carried away with the idea of a consumer revolution – the paintings and engravings of markets, books and clothes tempt you into making strong statements about this phenomenon. But you recognise the need to stay open-minded, so you pull back and ask a question instead: how important was this consumption in the economic growth in England during this period? *This gives you a fourth area to raise* and that seems plenty. You develop your presentation around the following:

- The historical debate about whether there was a consumer revolution.

- The nature of consumption in the period. What was the range of goods and why that particular range?

- The question of who did the consuming and the extent to which regions differed.

- The importance of home demand as a factor in economic growth. Was it crucial? How did it compare with foreign demand? Or with other factors?

The presentation can be structured as a brief discussion of these areas and you can raise a question, with your own thoughts for each. You will indicate at the start that there are four areas to your presentation and write up the names of your sources on the white board. The illustrations will serve as an ice-breaker for discussion as well as underlining your points.

What about your script? It helps to write very clearly and large enough for you to follow your own notes easily. This also helps with nerves. You could use a separate large record card for each of the four points and write a heading with sufficient notes to talk from. Or you could script every single word. Do what makes you comfortable, but practise different approaches as time goes on. Talking from notes sounds more natural than reading a text and should enable you to have more eye contact with the group.

How do you handle questions? This is another valuable skill to develop. Some people don't like the idea of having to answer any question that may come up because they won't have a chance to look anything up or think for very long about it. If you need time to think, try repeating the question, writing it up on the board or asking the questioner to clarify it. You are not expected to be an instant expert and, if you don't know, it is best to say so. But you can invite other students to contribute and see if you can broaden participation in discussion. When you do answer, try to look round the group and not just at the tutor or the person who asked the question. This also broadens out discussion.

Taking part in a discussion

When we talk to friends we have many small signals to help the conversation to flow. If we want to know something, we can simply say, 'What did you think about . . .?' or volunteer an opinion as a way of getting a response. We use all kinds of 'conversational glues' – the 'ers', 'ums' and 'you knows' of conversation – to keep things going and encourage them along. A seminar is formal, even when it is relaxed and we are not freewheeling in the same way. It might help you to know that academics have stock phrases or gambits that are designed as 'discussion signals' too. Here are some you might find useful to try (note how helpful it is to know names): 'When Joanne was talking about . . ., I wondered whether . . .'; 'Can we go back to the point we were discussing earlier when . . .?'; 'In the lecture we were told . . . But I don't see how . . .'; 'One of the things that puzzled/interested me was . . .'; 'From what I've read, I don't see how we can say . . .'.

My guess is that you will find these kinds of 'links' artificial and a bit of a strain at first. They *are* artificial. But so are many of the ways we operate through talk. Think of formal meetings with their 'Matters arising', 'Any other business' and the need to talk to other people round the table through the chairperson. Or think of Parliament and the rules it uses for debate. Or think of the meeting of any society, club or group you belong to. There are ways of getting into the conversation in all of these, and ways of killing the debate or keeping it alive. The aim of all the gambits I've suggested is to keep it alive by pushing the discussion further. Some students (and tutors) measure the success of a seminar by the heat generated; and, indeed, strong discussion can be stimulating and enjoyable. But in history seminars much more is likely to be achieved if a wide range of evidence and a number of different interpretations can be weighed and judged even-handedly.

A NOTE ON GROUP PROJECTS
by Tony Kirby

Historians are by tradition and nature solitary animals: as in all humanities subjects, the individual scholar toiling in the library or archive is the archetypal figure. Most history books and articles in learned journals are single-authored, in contrast to the natural sciences where collaboration between three or four authors is the norm.

But there are changes afoot, at all levels. Increasingly, academic historians (those who teach you) are being urged by the funding bodies to collaborate with others (and people working in other disciplines) to gain the all-important research grants. And at under-graduate level working with others is an essential 'transferable skill' that you can take into the world of employment and is thus recommended by the 2007 History Benchmark Statement.

In practice, you're almost certainly 'collaborating' with other students already, both informally (discussing your latest essay over a cup of coffee or online, working out what on earth Kirby was talking about in this morning's lecture) and more formally in seminars and tutorials.

But working together on a group project is a rather different matter.

First steps: getting started

- What sort of group are you in: self-selected or selected by your tutor? In the former case, internal dynamics should be non-problematic. In the latter, especially in larger institutions where you may not know many of your fellow-students well, you'll probably need an ice-breaking session.

- What sort of task have you been set? Is it a question (e.g. What distinguished middle-class houses in Victorian Britain?) or more open-ended (e.g. a topic such as 'the Victorian Country House'), leaving you to frame your own questions?

- Finding a time to meet might be a challenge. But it's a challenge you must rise to. Get several meetings into the group's diaries. It's easier to cancel a meeting than to arrange an extra one, especially if there is anyone in your group with a part-time job, a long journey to campus or a child to get home to.

- Begin by brainstorming. Some ideas will be runners, others won't. Even the latter might be resurrected at a later stage, so ensure one of the group keeps a careful note of what you've come up with.

- Who's going to do what? Allocate tasks according to interests and expertise. You will probably need an anchorman or woman: someone who will introduce the topic (and the 'performers'), act as a link between the different 'turns' and sum up at the end.

- Don't hide your light under a bushel: if you think you have a particular skill to offer, make this clear at your initial meeting.

- The audience: you'll be presenting to your fellow students. What level of knowledge of the topic can you assume? How many people will there be?

- This might dictate your mode of presentation: the more senses of your listeners you can engage, the better. Should you use transparencies and/or handouts, or PowerPoint? If you opt for it, think carefully about how you use PowerPoint. Don't put the full text of your presentation on the screen and read it out: otherwise you might just as well give everyone the print-out. Bullet-point headings are much better and give you the chance to expand on the topic naturally. Whatever medium you use, try to incorporate maps, photographs and the like in your presentation.

How's it going?

- Pulling your weight: this is a difficult one. What do you do about 'passengers'? First of all, make sure as a group that everyone has an equal role to perform (back-stage or front-stage). And don't forget that peer pressure works wonders.

- If you have a determinedly uncooperative or lazy person in your group, you may find yourself having to carry them for the sake of the group as a whole. This is especially infuriating when a group presentation is assessed and everyone is awarded the same mark. The only consolation is the value employers place on teamwork – that includes coping with awkward work colleagues and covering in emergencies, when someone in your team is absent for a genuine reason. If you claim team-working skills in a job application, you might be asked to describe how you would respond when things were not going well.

- A dress rehearsal is crucial: you need to have an idea of timing and pace (and that your visual aids will work as planned). You also need to build in time for questions and discussion afterwards. Provide prompts to help your audience devise questions. You might even 'plant' a question to set the ball rolling.

And on the day ...

- Nerves are natural and your tutor will know this: every time any of your tutors delivers a lecture (and I don't think I'm giving away any trade secrets here), he or she has 'butterflies'. But you will be amazed how, once you start, the adrenalin flows: 'There's no business like show business'.

- Finally, and easier said than done: don't just read out your script with your head buried in it. Adopt a 'natural' delivery style – you can be less formal than in writing an essay.

And finally ...

You have several years to practise the skills outlined in this chapter, to experiment and to try out different approaches. What seems like an ordeal at first will get easier, and can become a source of pleasure as you realise how much you have learned – not only as an historian but as a communicator.

7 Writing assignments

Mary Abbott

Ten years ago, this chapter would have been called 'Essay writing' but, while essays remain the apprentice historian's core task, students today encounter a variety of assignments: reviews of books, films, websites or reports on fieldwork, for example.

Students can be remarkably conservative. The essay is a familiar sort of assignment and many students are wary of novel tasks. Take comfort: the underlying principles are the same. See variety as a bonus rather than a stumbling block: when you leave 'the groves of academe', you may well be asked to write a proposal, a report, an evaluation or an executive summary. Unless you become a columnist for, say, *The Guardian* or *The Spectator*, you will not be asked to write an essay. Adaptability is a selling point – be glad that your skills are transferable.

Assignments, whatever their form, are not burdens imposed on student victims as a cruel rite of initiation into the historian's craft. They enable you (as well as your tutors) to test your understanding, judgement and application. They provide your tutor with opportunities to make constructive comments that should enable you to improve your performance and, ultimately, one hopes, achieve a 'good degree'. What's more, the skills acquired through writing assignments are skills in demand in the world of work: diligence, judgement, controlled imagination and the capacity to persuade, which of course requires good communication skills.

The process

An assignment is, or should be, the outcome of a complex, intellectually demanding and time-consuming process involving a number of linked elements:

*   investigation
*   evaluation
*   decoding the task
*   planning an academic argument
*   drafting
*   presentation and editing

and, finally,

*   digesting feedback from the person who has marked it.

Except for the final stages, the order is not immutable. There is a strong case for investigating or, as students often tag it, doing the 'research' before focusing down on the specific task. Pressure of time or the need to get through an unpalatable but unavoidable task can put 'decoding the task' at the head of the agenda.

Pace yourself. Given that few students are keen examinees, it is puzzling that so many students claim that they can only write assignments when they are working against the clock. This way of working is unwise. Whatever they did during their own apprenticeship, academics, in their judicial capacity, act on the premise that students work steadily through the term or semester. Having left yourself too little time to complete all your assignments is not an acceptable excuse.

Investigation

Students almost always receive guidance in the shape of a list of required or recommended resources, including reading. Many assignments require students to examine controversial issues. A good recent general book will provide you with grounding in the subject and a survey of the views of rival schools of interpretation. Thus briefed, you can dig deeper and tackle the specialists' contributions.

When reading for an assignment, it is generally wise to begin by skimming. At this stage, full notes are rarely a sound investment, but do take time to mark your trail: record the numbers of the pages along with a word or phrase to remind you of what caught your attention.

Note ideas as well as facts. Make sure that you can trace your notes back to their sources. Be scrupulous in your use of quotation marks and references to distinguish the words you have copied from your commentary on them. Plagiarism – the theft of other people's research, ideas or expressions (see Chapter 1, p. 9) – is perhaps the most serious academic crime and, if detected, is likely to be punished severely. Both crime and detection are much easier in our electronic age than in the days of print. Lazy, hasty and inarticulate students find downloading faster than composing and typing. Plagiarised passages often shine out like gems in the dross of a student's prose. Google can track stolen phrases down in seconds. Some universities routinely employ electronic detection systems.

STORAGE AND RETRIEVAL

It is worth experimenting with formats and methods of storage to discover what suits you best: it might be paper in a ring-binder, record cards in a box or electronic files on a disc. The word 'retrieval' is key. However you store your notes, the raw material for your assignment, you must be able to find your way around them. And you must be able to make sense of your notes when you come back to them after a gap. Notes should be significantly shorter than the text on which they are based. If, for some reason, you need the whole text, photocopy or download it.

Evaluation

If you engage effectively with your material, you will weigh up the evidence as you gather it. It is, however, important to stand back and take careful stock of the material you have accumulated – to find the gaps. But, if you tend to be the kind of investigator who finds it hard to stop digging, beware. At every stage in the process, it is important to remind yourself that you have to do the best you can in the time you have.

Decoding the task

Tutors invariably mark down work that is poorly focused. Translating the task into your own words is a good way of testing whether you have grasped what it entails. And it may help you to structure your assignment.

Titles generally include a command:

- assess
- criticise
- discuss
- evaluate
- review.

Each of these imperatives could be replaced by the instruction: use your judgement. The second, unwritten command is 'convince me'.

Planning an academic argument

The planning stage is one that you skimp at your peril. If you make a detailed plan, you free up all your energies for the vital and demanding task of translating your plan into continuous prose.

Recognise that academic arguments rarely conclude with a clear-cut, incontrovertible verdict. Remind yourself that our evidence is patchy and often biased. Lack of certainty fuels debate; it is one of the things that make history fun.

It is important to set your argument in its historical context. To put this as simply as possible, locate your topic in time and space. This may mean commenting on the physical environment; beliefs and values; social, economic and political structures and institutions; or the technologies of the period in question. It also involves demonstrating an awareness of the historiography – the work of the academic historians on whose shoulders you stand.

Hindsight is a dubious asset: to assume outcomes were inevitable is a grave mistake; partisanship is to be avoided. Your personal sympathies with those whose opportunities, civil rights or material circumstances were adversely affected by race, rank or gender must not be allowed to colour your evaluation. A good student adopts a clinical objectivity; a partisan produces polemic – a rant. An educated scepticism is the hallmark of an historian. Yet well-founded speculation may not be out of place. It is an aspect of the hard-to-pinpoint flair that lifts work into the First Class.

There is no single winning formula for a successful academic argument. Originality, as I have said, is a mark of First Class work. But perhaps the most common – and safest – approach to an assignment on a controversial theme is to put both (or all) sides of the debate systematically and even-handedly and conclude that there is something to be said for each of the positions. Although the historiography – the debates that have taken place between the historians who have interpreted and reinterpreted the topic of your assignment – is likely to be a key component of most assignments, don't confine yourself to pitting one set of authorities against another. Provide evidence: give specific examples to illustrate your argument.

Even if you agree or disagree strongly with a proposition, and have the evidence to support your case, invest some words in demolishing the opposing point of view.

The way you lay out your plan, on paper or on screen, is a matter of personal preference. Many students feel most at home working towards a series of statements written one beneath the other, like the sub-headings that punctuate articles in a newspaper. Experts on study skills generally advocate an approach that produces a plan resembling a spider's web or the trunk, branches and twigs of a tree. This strategy makes it easier to group evidence and slot in additional points than a pen-and-paper list. Experiment to see what works best for you.

Drafting

Like anyone else who writes for a living – the academic, the advertising copywriter, the journalist – you should consider your target reader. In your case the reader to keep in mind is not your tutor but a novice as far as this topic is concerned, a novice who is interested, intelligent and sceptical. You should not take expert knowledge and understanding of the topic for granted or discount what you have learned from lectures and discussions in class.

It would, however, be foolish to ignore what you know about your tutor. Shrewd students soon become skilled judges of their tutors' characters. Is the tutor who is going to mark your assignment open to ideas, invariably eager to promote debate? Or do students get their heads bitten off if they challenge views set forth in lectures? Most tutors sit somewhere between these extremes.

Assignments should be written in formal, though not pompous, English. Getting on for 300 years ago, Daniel Defoe, better known as the author of *Robinson Crusoe* (1719), offered excellent advice on writing in his *Complete English Tradesman* (1726). He urged his readers

> to write a plain and easy style. If any man was to ask me which would be supposed to be a perfect style or language, I would answer that in which a man speaking to five hundred people, of all common and various capacities, idiots or lunatics excepted, should be understood by them all.

He warns against 'ostentation', 'all exotic sayings, dark and ambiguous speakings, affected words . . . abridgements or words cut off'.

As you read, learn from the strengths and weaknesses of more practised writers. You will observe that some historians' arguments are crystal clear, fluent and persuasive; other academics produce pretty impenetrable prose. Get into the habit of reading serious newspapers and magazines – especially the editorials and the work of columnists who offer 'opinions' in essay form; and the book reviews and obituaries with an eye to style and structure. Write. Assignments tend to be bunched towards the end of the term or semester; try to make writing a part of your regular routine: keep a journal; review the books and articles you read.

Although professional historians who appear on radio and television frequently use the historic present – 'it is 1837, the young Victoria has just ascended her throne . . .' assignments should be written in the past tense.

Presentation and editing

The computer makes it easy to produce a professional-looking text. Use 12 point and an unfussy font such as Arial or Times New Roman. Unless you are instructed to do otherwise, set wide margins and double-space your text. Indent and single-space long quotations. The computer's spell-checker will help you to correct misspellings and eliminate 'typos', but keep an eye on it: the first word it selects may not be the one you want. It may not detect that you have typed 'open' when you intended to put 'pen' or 'exerts' when you meant 'experts' or even as gross an error as 'grammar phone'. Defer to the older generation's prejudices about punctuation: tutors find the omission and misuse of the apostrophe particularly vexing. Handing in work with mistakes of that kind is the academic equivalent of turning up for an interview with your flies undone or your skirt tucked into your knickers.

If you illustrate an assignment with maps, images or tables, put them where their impact will be greatest, not in an appendix but facing the text they complement. If you use material made by someone else, you must acknowledge this in the form required by your institution. You can use your own sketches, as long as they are clear and neat.

This is the moment at which you step out of the role of writer and into the shoes of your imaginary ideal reader – open-minded and responsive but alert and critical. It is hard to be thoroughly self-critical when you are struggling to meet a deadline. Indeed it could make a difficult situation worse. So try to manage your time so that you can return to your draft after a few days to review the structure of your argument, the robustness of the evidence you have used to support it and the clarity of your expression with a fresh eye. The computer has revolutionised our capacity to cut, insert and rejig text. Make use of it.

Does the evidence stand up to scrutiny? Do the links in the chain of argument bear the weight of your conclusion? Is it easy to follow? (Think how annoying poor signposting on an unfamiliar road or campus can be.) Make sure that you have flagged your key points and indicated what you plan to do next:

- *for instance* introduces evidence;
- *similarly* flags corroboration;
- *but, however* and *on the other hand* signal qualifications;
- *thus* and *in consequence* tell your reader that you are coming to the end of a section of your argument.

The finished product

- Introduction
- Conclusion
- Referencing

Introduction

Now is the time to write your introduction. Follow the example of the journalist rather than the writer of a whodunit. Use the introduction to summarise your argument and to explain why you have tackled the question in the way you have, for example why you have stressed some aspects at the expense of others.

Conclusion

The essential job of the conclusion is to remind your readers that you have done what was asked of you, weighed up the evidence and, very often, come up with a tentative, provisional answer. The conclusion offers the confident and well-informed student a chance to end with a flourish to open the question up and suggest that, given the opportunity, she could develop the argument to embrace a wider timescale or a bigger geographical area.

Referencing

Adhere scrupulously to the guidelines issued by your institution.

Feedback

Feedback comes in at least two varieties: marks and comments. Marks are banded into classes: First, Second – generally divided into Upper Second (2.1) and Lower Second (2.2), and Third. A First Class mark is 70 or above; a 2.1 between 60 and 69; a 2.2 between 50 and 59; a Third between 40 and 49. Work awarded fewer than 40 marks has failed to achieve Honours standard.

There is general agreement about the characteristics associated with degree classification in history. Anonymous submission, internal moderation and the scrutiny of External Examiners help to ensure that marking is fair.

First Class work

First Class work is characterised by some, or all, of the following qualities:

- wide and adventurous reading and, where appropriate, use of visual or material evidence;
- a sophisticated grasp of issues;
- a confident command of context;
- penetrating analysis;
- originality;
- cogent, cumulative argument, fully supported and documented;
- fluent writing style;
- comprehensive and accurate referencing.

Marks above 80 are awarded very sparingly indeed.

Upper Second Class work

Like a First, a 2.1 is a good degree. Upper Second Class work often has some First Class qualities but they are displayed only intermittently. It is marked by some or all of the following qualities:

- thorough familiarity with a wide range of source material;
- a sound grasp of context;
- a good focus on the question;
- good analysis;
- a well-developed argument;
- an array of detailed, relevant evidence;
- a good level of literacy;
- accurate referencing.

Lower Second Class work

Though not what an employer would call a 'good degree', a 2.2 is far from a bare pass. It is characterised by some, or all, of the following characteristics:

* dependence on a restricted range of materials;
* a limited understanding of context;
* adequate analysis;
* a good but incomplete response;
* an adequate argument;
* a patchy array of evidence;
* an adequate writing style;
* accurate referencing.

Third Class work

Third Class work is weak but still of Honours standard. It demonstrates some, or all, of the following characteristics:

* use of a limited range of materials;
* a poor understanding of context;
* limited analysis;
* a lack of focus on the task;
* a weak argument;
* inadequate evidence;
* poor use of English.

Failed work

Work fails for a variety of reasons. A mark of zero is normally awarded only to students who fail to submit an assignment or for plagiarism.

Assignments rarely display indicators of Class consistently. Even a failing assignment can display First Class quality – in, say, wide and adventurous reading. Remember that marks are an indication of current achievement. Most first-year students perform well below their true potential. Your tutor's comments will highlight the strengths and weaknesses of your work. It is particularly galling to receive the comment: 'This is one draft away from a 2.1'.

Your work on an assignment is not complete until you have digested your marker's feedback. If you don't understand it, arrange a meeting. Take constructive criticism on board and your marks should improve. Many universities employ study skills specialists. Seek them out.

8 Examinations

Adrian Gregory

M uch of the advice that applies to essay and dissertation writing also applies to exams. It's a good idea to read or re-read Chapter 7 on writing assignments alongside this one.

What is the point of exams?

What is the point of exams? Many people dread them and even good examinees doubt whether they are the best way to test the student's skills, knowledge and understanding. It may comfort you to know that lecturers have asked themselves this question and much less weight is placed on exams now than used to be the case. The way in which work is assessed and, in particular, the balance between exams and continuous assessment varies from institution to institution. This may well be a factor that influences your choice. It may be possible to find a place that will enable you to achieve a history degree without taking any exams at all. Nevertheless, timed exercises still play an important part in most university schemes of assessment and the purpose of this chapter is, first of all, to explain why this is so and, second, to equip you in order to improve your exam performance.

The case for exams

Although it may come as a surprise to some of you, there is a very good case to be made for exams. The examination system was originally devised in the interests of fairness: in the nineteenth century exams replaced patronage and purchases as the means of selecting candidates for the Civil Service and officers for the Army. In consequence, the senior civil servants who ran the Indian Empire in the second half of Queen Victoria's reign included the sons of gamekeepers, butchers and bakers, tailors and shoemakers, upholsterers and undertakers. Benjamin Jowett, Master of Balliol, who owed his academic career to his success as an examinee – his father was a printer – regarded exams as a character test. Advocating competitive entry to the Indian Civil Service he wrote:

> For the moral character of candidates, I should trust partly to the examination itself. University experience abundantly shows that in more than nineteen cases out of twenty, men of attainments are also men of character. The perseverance and self-discipline necessary for the acquirement of any considerable amount of knowledge are a great security that a young man has not led a dissolute life.

Many of the same considerations still apply today. There is growing concern in universities about the danger of electronic plagiarism: work done under exam conditions is demonstrably the product of the candidate's own unaided effort. Also, the tutor's likes and dislikes are less likely to influence the marks he or she gives an anonymous exam script. Jowett's comments hold good: exams do test your capacity to keep calm, to work under pressure and think on your toes – abilities that are important in the rough old world of paid employment. This is what the political sketch writer, Matthew Parris, a journalist not uncritical of ministerial performances, wrote of the Scottish Secretary, Michael Forsyth, in October 1995:

Mr Forsyth listens to the questions, thinks on his feet, then gets properly to grips with it . . .

He leaps at the Dispatch Box, confident of his intellectual mastery, unafraid of what anyone may throw at him, because he understands his own argument. He speaks in a coiled, measured, very slightly menacing way, as though dictating . . .

Hansard reporters will need little work on a Forsyth answer: the phrasing, the grammar, the balance of subordinate clauses – almost the punctuation – are all there.

In other words, his performance at the Dispatch Box has all the hallmarks of a 'good examinee'.

And don't forget that exams can save you time, a very precious commodity for those of you with family responsibilities, part-time jobs or other outside commitments – sport, theatre, student journalism, etc.

Exam formats

As we've already pointed out, exams have changed since Jowett's day. In recent years some tutors have been thinking hard about the ways in which they assess their students, designing methods to fit the particular range of knowledge, skills and understanding that they are seeking to develop in students taking a particular course or module. As a result, undergraduate exams come in different shapes and sizes and, although it is not yet extinct, the traditional end-of-year three-hour marathon, which requires you to tackle three or four unseen essay questions, is no longer the dominant form. Many conventional essay-based exams are now shorter. In modular systems they may occur at the end of a term or the end of a semester. In other words, there will be exams two or three times a year. Other exams depart from the old model in more radical ways. You may be allowed to take set texts or other material into the examination hall. You may get advance warning of the questions. If this happens, unless you have a photographic memory, do not attempt to write an essay in the usual less pressured way and learn it off by heart. You may find yourself sitting exams designed, for example, to test your under-standing of political ideas by inviting you to comment on an extract from *Das Kapital*, or your knowledge of the political geography of the Habsburg Empire by asking you to add the missing names of cities, states and rivers to a map of the world.

Preparing for exams

Whatever the format, the same general advice applies. Success in exams, as in other kinds of test, is most likely to be the reward of the canny candidate, who identifies and practises the essential techniques. Think of the amount of time and effort people put into practising for their driving test. The same principles apply to academic exams. Find out what is required of you. Practise. Don't wait until the last minute to revise. In some modular schemes there may be little or no time between the end of teaching and the start of the examination period. Even if there is a gap for revision, it is good practice to consolidate your knowledge and understanding as you go along.

Three key aspects of preparation are:

- making use of past papers
- active revision
- coping with stress.

Making use of past papers

Past papers *can't* be used to predict which topics the examiner will select. However, if they are used correctly, past papers are an invaluable asset to the exam candidate, so much so that, if there are no past papers, you should ask your tutors to provide a sample paper. When you use past papers, it is important to make yourself aware of the rubric – the local rules that apply to a particular exam: *how many and what sort of questions are you required to 'attempt'*, to use the classic and depressing language of the examiner? Check that the rubric isn't about to change. 'Failure to observe the rubric', by doing too many questions or too few or by muddling the regulations for sectionalised papers, may lead to the failure of an otherwise well-prepared candidate.

There are other good reasons for making yourself familiar with past papers. Papers set on an earlier occasion give a good idea of the *range and style of questions* you will face. If you are preparing yourself to sit a three-question paper, you should have a minimum of five topics you would be able to tackle.

Active revision

When you have chosen your topics, it is time to begin to gear yourself up for the exam. Reread your notes but don't sit hunched over your file. Make this an active process. Highlight or underline key facts (the names of the authorities you'll want to cite as well as, for instance, dates) and the key ideas. You may find it helpful to produce a condensed version of your notes on record cards.

Reading something new can help to freshen up your thinking – a book review from a broadsheet newspaper, *The Times Higher Education Supplement* or *Literary Supplement* or the *London* or *New York Review of Books* (all almost certainly available in your institution's library) won't take you long to get through and might pay big dividends in the form of new ideas and at least two names to drop into an exam answer: 'As Marks argued in his blistering review of Spencer's . . .'. If you are confident that you know who your examiners will be and what their prejudices are, you can, of course, adjust your wording to suit. 'As Marks alleged in his blistering review of Spencer's otherwise well-received . . .' might go down better.

Back to the past papers yet again. If you collect all the questions on, say, Irish Home Rule set over a period of five or six years, you can test both your *all-round knowledge and understanding* of the topic and your *ability to select what is relevant* to a particular question. The most effective way of doing this is by making answer plans. The challenge of making plans may expose gaps in your knowledge or understanding that you may need to plug. A student who can *plan a good response quickly* (by which I mean in five or six minutes) is at a tremendous advantage in an exam (and, as the example of Michael Forsyth suggests, this is a valuable asset in real life too). Brainstorming and refining answer plans is one element of preparation that you can usefully do with other people who are facing up to the same exam. It is possible to have a good time gearing up for exams with friends and a jar of coffee, some cans or a bottle of wine.

Learning to get an argument down on paper within the given time allowance is another vitally important skill – one you have, in the end, to develop on your own. The irresolute might experiment with the strategy that concentrates slimmers' minds so well and agree to *practise writing to time* with a support group of equally weak-willed friends. If possible, get a tutor to comment on what you produce. Alternatively, discuss the essays with your friends in the 'support group'. Remember that university exams are not like the old 11+. You are not in direct competition with each other.

Bear in mind that tutors may penalise you quite severely if you fail to *complete all the questions you are required to attempt.* Compensation for an unfinished answer is – quite rightly – regarded as unfair to the candidates who have delivered what they were asked for in the time allowed.

Knowing how much you can get down in *legible* handwriting in, say, 45 minutes will help you to scale your answer and allocate appropriate amounts of time to the different elements of the paper. *Illegible scripts irritate examiners.* If your handwriting is difficult to read, experiment with different instruments, try writing bigger, or join a calligraphy class. If there are genuine physical reasons for your inability to write legibly, your university should be able to make appropriate special arrangements by giving you access to a keyboard or providing you with an amanuensis or scribe. Obviously, tutors have to have advance warning of any special needs.

Coping with stress

Many undergraduates have learned to fear exams by going through the A level loop. At this stage of your education, the grade you get may seem to you, your parents and friends to be desperately important. After all it's what will decide whether or not you go to Footlights College, Oxbridge. Except for the minority aiming for research funding, degree results are much less significant in the long run. The class of your degree will certainly matter a great deal at the time the results come out but, once you've been out in the rough old world for a little while, only the 'university bore' will ask you 'what you got'.

   Of course, it pays to be sensible in the build-up to exams. Get into the habit of going to bed and getting up at conventional times and the thought of a nine o'clock exam won't be quite so daunting. Drink less alcohol – you won't give your best performance with a hangover. If you smoke, remember that you'll have to go without for the duration of the exam and condition yourself to appropriate gaps between cigarettes.

   For some students, fear of exams is so ingrained and acute that it is worth their while seeking professional help within the university. Tutors should be able to point you in the direction of someone skilled in teaching stress management and relaxation techniques.

The exam itself

Try to get a good night's sleep – revising all night won't help.

   Once you get into the exam room, the crucial first step is to *read the whole of the exam paper carefully*. Take as long as you need. Mark the questions you might attempt but don't start writing immediately. Students tend to waste time trying to read the examiner's mind before they have seen the paper but skimp the time they devote to reading it when they have it in front of them. Often an exam question is an invitation to discuss a well-known historian's views. You may be given a direct quotation followed by the instruction 'Discuss'. It is good practice for the examiner to identify the source of a quotation but you will be rewarded if you are able to demonstrate a knowledge of the writer in question in your answer. Sometimes the question will refer to the title of a book from the reading list, even the key text: 'Was mid-Victorian Britain an age of reform?'; 'Did the twentieth century see the rise of a professional society?'. You will score marks if you spot the reference.

If you are required to answer more than one question, *begin by writing the plan for both or all of them*. Remember that the best essays are the best-planned essays. You may find it helpful to start by jotting down as many points as you can think of but, of course, be prepared to discard everything that isn't strictly relevant to the question. It is better to end up with an essay that is well focused but on the short side than one that is obviously padded out with irrelevant material.

- A coherent argument, clearly expressed and well supported, will stand out from the scripts cobbled together in a panic.
- Evidence that you have thought for yourself will impress.
- Sketch maps and diagrams may help to explain complex arguments.

Don't allow yourself to be distracted from your commitment to *relevance*. Confront the question head-on. Whatever happens, don't change your mind part of the way through.

Show what you know. Dates and relevant accurate statistics look good. So do direct references to the historians you have read. At least as important is to demonstrate a *real grasp of issues* and an ability to put them *in context*.

Avoid anachronistic moral judgements. Reconstructing the thinking of a seventeenth-century witch hunter or a nineteenth-century trades unionist is an important part of the historian's trade.

Begin with an *introduction* setting out the key points in your argument. Just like their candidates, examiners are working under pressure and need all the help you can give them in following your argument.

End with a *conclusion*. Your conclusion may be a firm 'yes', a firm 'no' or – as often as not – a firm 'maybe'. The conclusion is the ideal place for a final flourish. Take the opportunity to suggest that there are other, and potentially more interesting, angles on the topic, demonstrating that you have read or thought about related issues that you have not been invited to address on this occasion. Now is your chance to use the best of the ideas you had to discard at the planning stage.

Between the introduction and the conclusion comes the *argument*. There are three basic approaches: the two most common build up to the historian's usual firm 'yes' or 'no' or 'maybe'.

'*Strong assertion*' is a more pretentious way of describing the firm 'yes' or 'no'. If you take this line, you will concentrate on marshalling evidence and theoretical reasons in support of your contention. Either way, you will need to make at least a passing reference to the opposing point of view, if only to demonstrate why you have concluded that it is absurd. Usually, you will need to spend time on the demolition job.

'*The classic dialectic*' is a more pretentious translation of the firm 'maybe'. You put the case for both sides fairly, pointing out the strengths and weaknesses. You probably end up sitting on the fence. Or, if you are able, you may come up with an alternative conclusion of your own.

The third and by far the riskiest approach is to *question the question*. For this strategy to succeed, you need to be able to demonstrate that you have understood the question and could, if you wanted, produce a conventional argument – rather like the artist who can produce highly competent representational works but chooses not to. To adopt this strategy, you need to be confident that you have 'star quality'.

Whatever the pressure, resist the temptation to adopt what we might call the 'Blue Peter' strategy and produce an answer you prepared earlier. The odds against it precisely fitting a question your tutors have devised makes the National Lottery look like a racing certainty. And try to avoid being reduced to incoherence. The result is the intellectual equivalent of what Barry Humphries used to describe as the 'technicolor yawn' – spewing up all you can remember about a topic in a thoroughly messy way. If you find yourself seized by panic in the middle of an exam, it may help to stop writing, put your pen down and look out of the window to a world outside the exam room until you calm down again. After all, there are more important things than exams.

9 The dissertation or major project

Tony Kirby

Almost every undergraduate history course in the UK requires you to write a dissertation, a thesis or a major project in your final year. This will almost certainly be your most substantial single piece of written work and may seem a daunting prospect. It shouldn't, because the rather forbidding History Benchmark Statement's requirement that history students should, towards the end of their course, 'formulate, execute and complete an independent extended piece of written work' is your opportunity to be a 'real' historian.

Why 'real'? Because most undergraduate written work is really a form of literary criticism: you're being asked to assess, analyse and compare what the 'professionals' have written on historical topics (usually quite narrowly defined) in response to questions set by your tutors. Time pressures alone mean that you're unlikely to have the luxury of going beyond this and looking at the sources (written and other) that they've used.

The dissertation gives you independence in your *choice* of topic, how you *research* it and how you *write* it. It's the culmination of your undergraduate career and, even if you never write anything else on history in the rest of your life, the skills that you acquire or refine in producing it – marshalling evidence, managing information and making a convincing case – will be invaluable in whatever career you pursue.

Choosing a topic

It's never too early to start thinking about this: even in your first year, keep an eye open for possible areas to investigate. You may already have made your mind up, if there's a period that you're passionately interested in: the English Civil War for example. But, even here, you'll have to refine your topic and choose a specific aspect to home in on.

It's more likely that you'll have several possibilities in mind, probably falling into one or more of the following categories:

*   A *historical controversy* that you want to investigate more fully: for example, how 'cruel' was the New Poor Law?
*   An *episode* touched on in your course that you'd like to explore in detail: for example, the Versailles Settlement.
*   Something *local or regional*: for example, the history of your own town or village.
*   Something *thematic*: perhaps an interest independent of the academic course you have followed, for example railways, cars, defence works or fashion.
*   If you're combining history with another subject, you might want to use *the expertise you've acquired in both*, such as the value of a novel as a historical source: for example, how useful is Winifred Holtby's *South Riding* (1936) to the historian of inter-war Britain?

In making your decision, there are several practical points to bear in mind:

*   *The project must sustain your interest and engagement over a lengthy period*: it should not become a chore.
*   *The project has to be feasible*. This means finding out, at a very early stage, what source materials are available: there's no point in choosing a topic only to discover that it will prove impracticable through lack of information.

- *You should establish where your likely sources are located.* If you're located outside London, a topic involving a lot of research in the National Archives at Kew is probably a non-starter, because of the time and expense involved (but don't ignore the website). This doesn't mean that you should abandon the idea: rather, cast round for alternative approaches. For example, if you have a passionate interest in railways, investigating their impact on Victorian social and economic life through local newspapers, directories and the like would be much more feasible than wading through the voluminous records of the railway companies deposited at Kew.

- *Accessibility may be a problem.* For example, if you want to work on the history of your home area, but are studying elsewhere, will there be sufficient time during vacations to collect the material you need? You may well have a job, which will cut down the time you can study; additionally, libraries and record offices may be closed for a lengthy period over Christmas and the New Year. You can use online sources for local studies (e.g. the Census), but you may have to pay to access these (although free access is often available via local libraries and record offices).

- *Bear in mind the availability of sources in English,* if you're thinking of a non-British or American topic.

- *You should also check your institution's ethical guidelines* if you are intending to undertake research using live subjects – an oral history project, for example.

Finally, the topic must be one in which there's some *academic expertise* in your History department: there has to be someone who can 'supervise' (guide) your progress and assess the dissertation at the end of the day. After the first 18 months of your course you should have a good idea of staff interests (and many departments publish a list of these: lecturers' areas of specialism aren't necessarily restricted to those that they teach). Try to build up a good relationship with your supervisor from the start: he or she can save you from pitfalls, suggest source materials and (probably) read a proportion of the dissertation before it's submitted. The supervisor is unlikely to be impressed if your first contact is a week before the dissertation is due in.

Next steps

Assuming that you've identified your sources and know that you can gain access to them, you then need to *refine your topic* and, eventually, come up with a *title*. It's best to start with quite a wide canvas: it's far easier to narrow down a topic when you discover that there's more material than you can comfortably cope with than to broaden out from a narrow basis. And, if you do slim down, this doesn't mean that your preliminary work will be wasted: it will give you a context into which to put the material you do eventually decide to use, even if you don't refer to it directly, and this will show through in the finished dissertation.

Word limits vary, but the limit set by your institution will give you some indication of how wide your scope can be. A limit of 10,000 words equates to only four 'standard' essays – you will need an Introduction and a Conclusion too, of course. Following on from this, if you think of each chapter as an essay, you're going to end up with three, or at most four. So you'll only be able to deal satisfactorily with three or four aspects of your topic. You won't know what these are until you've started your research, but within a relatively short time you should start to get some idea of what the eventual shape of the dissertation is likely to be and this will help to determine the direction of your work from that point onwards. Don't, under any circumstances, attempt more than four chapters: if you do, not only will the dissertation have a 'bitty' feel, but you'll find it difficult to develop a sustained argument in chapters only a couple of pages long.

So your topic has to be *manageable*. Avoid over-ambition: you may want to write something on the First World War. It would be impossible to cover the whole course of the conflict in

10,000 words – focus on a specific aspect, for example the impact of the war on an individual community as portrayed through the columns of the local press, or through war memorials.

Eventually, you will have to *propose a title*, probably round about October or November if your dissertation is due in the following May. You need to think carefully about this, and discuss possibilities with your supervisor. You will still have quite a lot of research to undertake, so avoid giving hostages to fortune if your research takes you in an unexpected direction by January or February.

One of the biggest problems may be the *time-span*. You will have to give some indication of this for your title to be accepted: the trick is to avoid being too precise, except where you're looking at a clearly defined episode. To return to the First World War, if you were investigating how the British press treated the build-up to Britain's involvement you would obviously be examining the period between 29 June and 4 August 1914. It's more difficult if you're looking at a topic that is open-ended, for example primary education in Victorian Britain: here, the best way forward would probably be to choose two significant pieces of legislation as your starting and finishing points, for example the 1870 and 1902 Education Acts. It's even more difficult if you're investigating the history of an individual community, but something like 'The social and economic development of Thetford in the nineteenth century' would be acceptable. The topic is anchored in space (it's about Thetford) and time (the nineteenth century). You might find that you end up concentrating on the mid-Victorian years, but so long as you put these in the broader context of Victorian Thetford, and explain in your Introduction why you've concentrated on the period you have done, your examiners should be satisfied.

Researching your dissertation

In some ways, this isn't very different from researching an essay, simply more extensive in scope and time.

Many institutions insist that you submit a preliminary bibliography towards the end of your second year. If yours does, follow Penny King's advice (see Chapter 4). The nature of the bibliography will obviously depend on the topic that you've chosen, but in most cases it will probably be a combination of primary and secondary sources. It will help you determine the feasibility of your research area and give you the opportunity to discuss with your supervisor sources you may have overlooked. There's usually no stipulation that you *should* use primary sources, especially if you're working on a non-British topic, but doing so (even if they're in translation) will add depth to your work (and impress your examiner).

There are many 'finding aids' and increasingly you can access these online. The usual caveats apply here: beware of personal websites that have a particular axe to grind. UK websites with an 'ac.uk' or 'org.uk' URL can always (in the case of the former) and usually (the latter) be trusted, as can US ones with an 'edu' tag.

Keep a precise note of *where you obtained your information*, for example the exact title of a book, the name of its author, the date and place of publication and the page numbers. For primary sources (documents), note the accession number. In the case of websites, give the date when you accessed the information, as websites can change their content or disappear completely.

Set yourself a calendar: what you hope to achieve, by when. Make it realistic – you are not going to be able to devote 100 per cent of your time to researching and writing your dissertation: you'll also have essays to write, seminars to prepare for (and also a life outside history to lead). Don't be discouraged if you don't adhere to it strictly, but try to do so on a longer-term basis (month to month). And, crucially, don't leave everything until the last possible moment. You may tell yourself that you work better under pressure. For an ordinary term essay this may be the case. For a dissertation it isn't.

How you *organise/keep your material* is a matter of personal preference, but, whatever you do, *don't* put it all on your PC (at least without back-up).

Finally, it's important to *know when to stop*. Research acquires an inbuilt momentum of its own, and if you're not careful you can carry on collecting more and more information. You simply need enough for your purpose, which is to present a coherent and well-supported argument. There will almost certainly be gaps in your knowledge and you would be wise to acknowledge these (see p. 106), but, if we all waited until we'd explored every possible avenue or never chanced our arm with an argument we think persuasive but can't fully support, we'd never write anything.

Everyone has his or her own way of working and I'm reluctant to be over-prescriptive here. But I would suggest that you start drafting your central three or four chapters as soon as possible. If you've had a good session in the library or the record office, give yourself time to reflect on the material you've gathered. After a day or two go back home, draft a couple of sentences, even rough out a chapter and you'll start to get some idea of what you know, what you don't yet know and still need to research.

Writing up

So you've gathered all your material and (hopefully) have a rough idea of how you're going to arrange it. All that now remains is the final writing up.

Before you start, check your institution's house rules: if you don't follow them, it's at your own risk. They will include *presentation* (for example, double-spacing for text), how to treat *quotations* (usually, if more than a set number of words, they are indented and single-spaced) and – crucially – the *word limit*: does this include quotations and footnotes?

If you treat the central three or four chapters like essays, they won't give you any problems: but remember that, as well as having its own internal argument, the first should lead the reader on to the next, and so on, to build up the *overall* argument. If you were writing about transport in Britain between the wars, for example, a chapter on cars, buses and lorries might end:

> Road transport thus was clearly emerging as a threat to the railways in the 1920s: the next chapter explores how effective were the companies' strategies for dealing with it.

Some technical points

Footnotes, *endnotes* and *referencing* will be subject to your own institution's rules: ignore these at your peril. If you are (perhaps unlikely) given a free hand as to how to do them, be consistent: don't mix footnotes and endnotes, the Harvard system of referencing with others, or have endnotes for some chapters but not others. And use notes for their proper purpose: to enable interested readers to follow up your sources. They should not to be used to get round the word limit.

Good English is crucial. Avoid slang and 'conversational' speech. In particular, a quotation is just that, and not a 'quote': the latter should only be used as a verb, as in 'Pugin, quoted by Rosemary Hill, *op. cit*, p. 98'. Incidentally, if your quotation comes from a published work, you should make this clear: it's only honest and the person transcribing it may just possibly have got it wrong. Railway stations are not 'train' stations (except in the USA) and 'enormity' is not a synonym for 'scale': 'the enormity of Nazi atrocities in the Ukraine' is correct; 'the enormity of the cotton industry by 1850' isn't. Split infinitives are to be carefully avoided as, although not incorrect, they lack elegance. Finally, it's essential that you use the apostrophe for its proper purpose.

Anachronisms include monetary values: inflation has robbed any pre-decimalisation (and indeed most twentieth-century) figures of any modern meaning. It is not helpful, for example, to convert the price of a loaf of bread in 1800 into present-day values. The important point is to put expenditure into the context of income.

I've started: how do I finish?

Anyone making any sort of presentation, written or oral, knows that there are two crucial requirements: getting your audience's attention at the outset, and leaving them feeling they've learned something at the end. Hence the importance of your Introduction and Conclusion.

The *Introduction* is vital, because it sets the scene for what follows and it's your chance to get the examiners on your side. Not only should it give an indication of the scope of the dissertation but, equally important, it offers the opportunity to say something about your approach in a more personal way than in succeeding chapters. For example, you could say something about what awakened your interest in the topic in the first place, the source materials you used and any problems you encountered. You can also explain here why you may have decided to concentrate on certain aspects of a much larger overall topic, for example:

> In researching the subject, it quickly became apparent that there was an embarrassment of material. There was no possibility of covering all aspects of the Yorke family's ownership of Wimpole from 1740 to 1890 in detail: thus this dissertation concentrates on their building and landscaping activities, although these are set throughout in the context of the national and local political, intellectual and social activities in which they were involved.

This shows your examiner that you're aware of the need to place your material in a wider framework, and that you have kept to the word limit. Note the word 'context': it's essential that you anchor your dissertation within a wider framework. This might be:

- *Historiographical*: essential if you're dealing with a topic that has been the subject of historical debate. Even if it hasn't (there is, for example, little debate over Victorian market towns), you need to survey the available literature on the subject.

- *Scene-setting*: if you're dealing with the local dimensions of a broader topic, you need to give the wider picture: a dissertation on Victorian public health in Wisbech that didn't look at the national legislative framework would justifiably be marked down.

- *Spatial*: again, for local topics you need to place your chosen community in its geographical and historical setting: whoever is reading your dissertation will probably not know this as well as you.

The danger is that context takes over. Use your common sense: how much does the reader need to know? Let's assume that you're writing about the Victorian copper industry of the Caradon area of East Cornwall:

- Tell your reader where Caradon is and outline its geography and geology.

- Write a paragraph (no more) on the Cornish mining industry in general.

- Explain why the copper industry enjoyed such a boom in the nineteenth century and why this was so short-lived.

- And, in this particular case (an early example of de-industrialisation), a scene-setting paragraph on what's to be seen today in a landscape of tourism would immediately 'hook' your reader.

This gives the necessary background to the detailed treatment of individual mining locations that might follow: you *don't* need to broaden your discussion out to a general economic and social history of Victorian Cornwall (although you could, with profit, mention this and refer to the appropriate sources in a note).

A word of advice: write your Introduction last. It's only when you've written the bulk of the dissertation that you'll know what are the salient points you wish to bring out.

The same applies to the *Abstract*, which often seems to give students trouble, perhaps through confusion between it and the Introduction. The purpose of the Abstract is simple: to summarise the scope, argument and contents of the dissertation, so that future readers will know immediately if it's relevant to their purposes. It usually has a tight word-limit (perhaps 300). It should give some indication of the sources used (but no detail), the argument of each chapter and the conclusions reached. For example:

This dissertation examines the rise of Whitby, North Yorkshire, as a holiday resort between 1830 and 1939. The Introduction places Whitby in its broader geographical and historical setting, and assesses the strengths and weaknesses of the evidence used (mainly local newspapers, maps and the Census) . Chapter 1 examines the changes brought about by the growth of the railway network and Chapter 2 how entrepreneurs, notably George Hudson, capitalised on the town's new-found accessibility in developing the 'West Cliff' area. Chapter 3 looks at the growth of the holiday trades and who provided them, and Chapter 4 explores inter-war Whitby, with particular reference to the battles between 'reformers', who wished to sweep away many of the Old Town's buildings, and 'conservationists', who believed this would destroy the resort's appeal. The Conclusion considers whether Whitby was a 'success' (compared to Scarborough, Filey and Bridlington) and tests it against 'models' of the growth of resorts in nineteenth- and twentieth-century Britain.

This is a very simple example – all academic journals carry abstracts of their articles: study them.

The *Conclusion* is equally important. It should summarise the argument of the preceding chapters and give some final thoughts, stressing the limitations of your research and suggesting future lines of inquiry. So, if your topic is 'The historical geography of the Sherlock Holmes stories', an example could be:

It has been possible to trace, from the Holmes canon, the geographical location of the vast majority of the stories and demonstrate Conan Doyle's detailed knowledge of the South London suburbs in particular. Nonetheless, uncertainties remain, notably the setting of *The Hound of the Baskervilles*, which appears to be an amalgam by Doyle of various localities in and around Dartmoor. And where in the Peak District was *The Priory School*; and why did Holmes set out from Euston rather than St Pancras to get there?

If nothing else, this will mean your examiners can't say 'It is unfortunate that the writer ignored such as aspects as . . .'. Showing that you have recognised the loose ends can only do you good.

For the *Bibliography*, once again, it's crucial that you check the house rules, but the standard running order is:

- Manuscript primary sources, listed alphabetically, by archive.
- Printed primary sources, listed alphabetically by author.
- Secondary sources, listed alphabetically by author, and divided between books and articles.

Take your supervisor's advice regarding other sources, such as oral interviews, broadcasts and films.

What else you include will depend on the nature of your topic: the only hard-and-fast rule is that any additional material must be directly relevant to the dissertation. The most usual are:

- *Maps*: crucial if you're writing about a specific town, village or region. For the Victorian period and after, Ordnance Survey 6-inch (1:10 560) and 25-inch (1:2 500) maps are essential and are available from record offices and libraries and in an increasing number of reprints. For a broader study, OS 1-inch maps are equally useful (and again, reprints are widely available), but you should bear in mind that, as these were revised very infrequently (and then only for minor changes) in the nineteenth century, they should be treated with extreme care as primary sources. But, for almost any topic, a map is helpful to the reader: if you're writing about the industrialisation of nineteenth-century Belgium, include a map of the country, showing all the places mentioned in the text and other information you consider useful. Don't overload the map, though: in this particular case, separate maps of the transport network and the Sambre/Meuse area would be needed.

- *Appendices*: as always, the relevance rule applies. They are not a dumping ground for material that might be of interest to readers but is not crucial to your argument. Use them sparingly: a good example would be a family tree, if you were writing about an industrial dynasty such as the Darbys of Coalbrookdale; a bad one would contain the whole text of the 1832 Great Reform Act if you were studying Parliamentary elections in the 1830s.

- *Illustrations* must be referred to in your text and, once again, must be relevant. Captions are usually exempt from the word limit (but you must check this!) and give you the opportunity to demonstrate your ability to analyse non-textual primary sources. Ideally, illustrations should be placed as near as possible to the appropriate point in the dissertation.

- *Statistics*: include these by all means (and incorporate them in the body of the text) but do not assume that they are self-evident: comment on what they purport to show, and what reliance can be placed on them.

- *Abbreviations*: a list of the most-used is helpful. In the text itself, you should write the name in full when you use it for the first time, e.g. 'Incorporated Church Building Society (ICBS)'. Thereafter, the initials alone will suffice. You might also consider a *Glossary* if your dissertation contains technical terms.

- A *chronology* is useful if you are dealing with a defined period (e.g. Napoleon's 'Hundred Days') and may help you to avoid large amounts of narrative in your text.

- *Acknowledgements* are a matter of common courtesy, but restrict them to those people who've helped you directly with your dissertation.

And finally . . .

Your dissertation should look like a professional piece of work. Ensure that it's correctly paginated, that it doesn't mix justified/ unjustified text, and that paragraphs are paragraphs and not single sentences. Ideally, complete your 'final' text at least ten days before the submission deadline: leave it for five, then reread it: you'll be amazed how many spelling mistakes and loose ends you find.

The dissertation is yours, more than any other piece of work you do in your History course. Enjoy it: remember that you can probably tell your examiners something they didn't know (or at least challenge their assumptions) and that it's not unlikely that other people will be using it at some point in the future to start them on their own research. There are few greater pleasures than seeing your own name in the footnotes and bibliography of someone else's publication!

Acknowledgements

This chapter owes much to the students whose dissertations I have supervised over the years and even more to the (unwitting) advice of two colleagues with whom I've shared supervision of both dissertations and other projects: Dr Mary Abbott (Anglia Ruskin University) and Dr Paul Richards (College of West Anglia).

The illustrative dissertation topics (and extracts) are purely that: but if they inspire anyone to follow up Sherlock Holmes, Whitby or Wimpole that would be a bonus!

10 Employability

Mary Abbott

The UK produces more than 9,000 history graduates a year. Only a minority move on to careers directly related to the subject.

Nevertheless, the historian's skills and qualities of mind open up a world of other opportunities. MI5 recruits historians. A leading design and engineering consultancy singles out History as one of the disciplines from which it prefers to select future management consultants. England's top woman chef is a history graduate.

Employers recruit men and women with good degrees in history – Firsts and Upper Seconds – because they can be confident that they have developed skills that can be deployed in a wide variety of settings. Some History Departments routinely explain the relevance to employability of the knowledge and skills fostered by their courses.

By the time you graduate, you should have

- learned to ferret out and weigh up evidence (research and analysis);
- gained experience in making a persuasive case (argument);
- developed strong communications skills – written and oral – *along with*

- the ability to come up with innovative ideas and solutions;
- the intellectual independence to defend them;
- teamworking skills;
- the capacity to work under pressure and meet deadlines.

One history graduate in five goes on to further study; one in ten for a higher degree – by no means all of these are in history. And even a budding academic needs employability skills.

Historians who go into 'graduate employment' can expect to be put on to their companies' Graduate Development Scheme. Those who go into 'unskilled' jobs in catering, supermarkets or department stores can, if they choose, transfer their history skills to these settings and use them to build careers in these industries.

The historian's options are so wide that it is worth enlisting as a career detective in your first year. Follow twin trails in tandem. Get to know your University Careers Service, not only an unrivalled source of information and expert advice on career choice, but also a coaching service that will help you to sell yourself effectively, on paper – in your *curriculum vitae* and application, and in person – at interview.

At the same time, widen your horizons through volunteering or a work placement. I'm using volunteering in its widest sense: helping to run the History Society – or the rowing club or the student newspaper; serving as a rep on a university committee; mentoring a child in danger of dropping out of school; or working in a night shelter for homeless people would all qualify as volunteering – and could help you to stand out from other 'good graduates' in history by demonstrating skills that enhance your employability. What's more, voluntary service, 'community engagement' or, as it is sometimes called, 'corporate social responsibility', is high on the agenda of many companies and of public sector employers who welcome recruits with a similar commitment.

If, like many history students, you have a fancy to work in a museum, a placement that takes you behind the scenes would enable you to test your dream against everyday reality and strengthen an application for a junior post or an MA in Museum Studies. Some universities have employer mentoring schemes, which pair students with experienced professionals who may or may not be employed in a field directly related to the student's subject.

Paid employment also provides useful experience. An evening job filling racks in a clothes shop, taken to pay off a first-term overdraft, led to a better-paid supervisory role and, nearing graduation, to the offer of a management training post (the graduate in question turned it down in favour of an MA in Military History). The holder of a senior university job began her career in university administration as a summer temp in the Admissions Office. The top woman chef worked in a restaurant while she was a student.

By comparison with the wider world of work, which welcomes history graduates with open arms, the entry gate to an academic career is narrow and the route to a permanent job is often long and arduous. A taught MA course might be the first step. (At Oxford and Cambridge, where graduates buy their MAs, the title Master of Studies (MSt) is used.) You would be more likely to embark on an MPhil, which involves a much larger element of supervised research and a longer dissertation in the hope and expectation of transferring your registration to PhD. A PhD is effectively a prerequisite for a university teaching post. Few full-time history research students complete their PhD within four years. Funding Councils ask referees whether applicants for bursaries to support their doctoral studies have achieved a spectacular once-in-a-generation First or just scraped into the First Class by the skin of their teeth. Historical research involves a great many solitary hours of reading in libraries and archives and writing up. This is a huge investment and, in career terms, the return is uncertain.

Fortunately, there are ample opportunities to keep your interest in history alive while you build a career in a different field. *Read*: keep in touch with the work of academic historians through a critical engagement with their books and articles. *Join*: the

Historical Association offers a bridge between academics and interested members of the public. It is especially important in the continuing professional development of people teaching history in schools. *Look*: your educated curiosity will enable you to get more out of visits to exhibitions and to historic sites, including public places such as St Pancras station, built to designs by Gilbert Scott in the 1870s to complement the train shed designed by William Barlow in 1863. *Do*: historical research need not be an expensive pastime. Valuable work can be done on material in a local studies collection near you.

11 Historical terms

Tony Kirby

This chapter attempts short definitions of some words and phrases that you may come across during your student career, under three headings:

- Political history
- Economic, social and cultural history
- Varieties of history and historical writing

together with notes on

- The British monetary system before decimalisation
- The Christian year.

The selection of terms, their allocation to each of the above categories and their definitions are intentionally idiosyncratic. Selection is based on the 'known unknowns' (those have troubled my own students over the years), allocation is arbitrary and the definitions are designed to make you think. My fellow contributors would challenge some, and so should you.

I have paid slightly more attention to the Christian faith (especially in Britain) than is usual, not least because ideas and practices remote to many of us today were central to most people's lives well into the twentieth century.

Note that cross-references, which may be to another section, are indicated by **bold italics**; other useful terms, whose meanings should be self-evident from the context, are *italicised*.

There's one obvious gap: past geographies and geographical terminology are largely ignored. The best investment you can make as a student (after buying this book) is a good historical atlas.

Abbreviations

Fr   French

Ger   German

Political history

Absolutism   Monarchical power unfettered by representative institutions. Usually applied to Western European monarchies of the seventeenth and eighteenth centuries.

Anarchism   Developed from the mid-nineteenth century: the view that society can be organised without the political apparatus of 'the state'. Should be distinguished from *anarchy*, which means the collapse of the apparatus of government.

Ancien Régime   Literally, 'old order' *(Fr)*. Strictly speaking, the political and social characteristics of France before 1789, but often applied more generally to the whole of Western Europe (including Britain 1688–1832).

Appeasement   The policy of British and French governments of the 1930s to meet the demands of Hitler and Mussolini through concessions and conciliation. Associated particularly with Neville Chamberlain (PM 1937–40) and culminating in the 1938 Munich

Agreement. Defended by some historians on the grounds that it was an attempt to avoid repetition of the horrors of the First World War, and that it bought time for Britain to commence rearmament, but for most remains – as it was at the time – a pejorative term.

Blitzkrieg/Blitz   Literally, 'lightning warfare' *(Ger)* as practised in the early years of the Second World War. Shortened form applied to German bombing of British cities (especially London, Coventry, Hull, Sheffield and Plymouth), from September 1940 to May 1941, and sometimes to the V1/V2 raids of 1944/5.

Christian Democracy   Political movement that can be traced back to the late nineteenth century, but achieved greatest prominence in post-1945 Western Europe. Anti-communist/socialist, it stresses individual freedom, a belief in the market economy (regulated where necessary) and moral conservatism (e.g. the sanctity of marriage, opposition to abortion), but couples this with support for the *welfare state*. Especially strong in Italy and Germany and in Spain after 1975 (the death of Franco).

Clarendon Code   Series of Acts passed by the post-Restoration 'Cavalier Parliament' (1661–79) to demote *Dissenters* (see *dissent*) to the status of second-class citizens. The most important were the Corporation Act, which excluded them from local government and the 1673/8 Test Acts (originally aimed at Roman Catholics and in particular the king's brother, James, Duke of York), by which non-Anglicans were excluded from all civil and military office and Parliament. In practice, they were able to participate in local government by *occasional conformity* (taking communion in the Church of England once or twice a year) and in Parliament due to annual passage of an Act of Indemnity from 1727 onwards.

Cold War   The post-Second World War confrontation between the Soviet Bloc (the *Warsaw Pact* powers) and *NATO*. At its most intense between 1947 and 1962 and again in the late

1970s/early 1980s. After 1985 relations eased markedly, and it was declared 'at an end' by Bush and Gorbachev in 1989.

Collectivism   A belief that some or all of the means of production and exchange should be 'collectively' owned for the national good, with the profits being shared by all. Often applied more generally to the State having a role to play in protecting the weaker members of society (see *welfare state*).

Comintern   Body established by the Soviet government in 1919 and used by the USSR to control the policies of foreign communist parties. Abolished 1943.

Communism   A political system based on the ideas of Karl Marx, in which (theoretically) the workers control the means of production.

Concert of Europe   Following the end of the Napoleonic Wars, it was hoped that the Great Powers (Austria, Britain, France, Prussia, Russia) could prevent future conflicts by acting together to prevent them spiralling out of control. Initially, this was to be achieved by regular 'Congresses'. Although by the early 1820s this had broken down, the Powers managed to defuse potentially inflammable situations (such as Belgian independence and neutrality) until the 1850s (the Crimean War) and periodically thereafter (e.g. the 1878 Congress of Berlin). Grey's 1914 abortive proposal for an international conference to avert world war seemed to see the end of the 'Concert', but the idea underlies all subsequent international bodies, such as the League of Nations and the United Nations.

Conscription   Compulsory military service.

Conservatism   Traditionally, a belief that, although political and economic structures should change in accord with evolving circumstances, changes should always also be in accord with a nation's past traditions.

Conservative Party   A new name for the *Tories*, first used officially by Peel in the 1834 *Tamworth Manifesto*. Not used for some years after Peel's fall (1846), it crept back into use in the 1870s.

Decolonisation   The process whereby the European powers divested themselves of overseas political responsibilities after 1945 under the twin pressures of nationalist movements in their colonies and a realisation of the costs of maintaining an imperial presence.

Democracy   Representative government based on a broad (e.g. nineteenth-century Britain) or universal (e.g. twentieth-century Britain) *franchise*.

Détente   Relaxation of international tension, especially in the *Cold War* period.

Devolution   The granting of self-government by a superior assembly (e.g. the Westminster Parliament) to a local one (e.g. the Welsh Assembly). Increasingly used in the twenty-first century as a catch-all phrase where derogation of powers occurs.

Dictatorship   Power wielded by a person/group, often of uncertain legitimacy, who/which may have achieved power by a *coup d'etat*.

Dual Monarchy   Austria–Hungary, 1867–1918.

Elector   With a capital 'E', the group of German princes (or high ecclesiastics) who elected the Holy Roman Emperor from the thirteenth century until 1806.

Enlightened Despotism   Despotism tempered by the ideas of the *Enlightenment*. Associated especially with Joseph II of Austria, Frederick the Great of Prussia and the Empress Catherine of Russia.

Fascism   Originally applied to the one-party state established by Mussolini in the 1920s, and subsequently to any right-wing movement combining total allegiance to its leader with a willingness to use brute force to gain and retain power. *Neo-Fascism*, stemming from unemployment, a sense of national decline and xenophobia, emerged in parts of Europe (e.g. Italy and the former East Germany) in the late twentieth century.

Fellow traveller   A communist sympathiser who is not actually a party member, particularly in Britain in the 1920s.

Franchise   The right to vote.

Imperialism   Empire-building. First used to describe the ambitions of Napoleon I, it achieved widespread currency after 1870 with the expansionist activities of the European powers and the USA. It is usual to distinguish between 'formal' imperialism (the direct political control of territory) and 'informal', where control is exercised indirectly, usually by economic means and with the cooperation of locally dominant classes, as by Britain in nineteenth-century South America.

Jingoism   Bellicose armchair imperialism. From a music hall song of 1878: 'We don't want to fight/But by Jingo if we do . . .'.

Labour Party   Founded 1900: its roots lay in the trade union movement and socialist societies of the late Victorian era, but it is generally regarded as owing more to Methodism than Marx. Replaced the Liberals as the alternative to the *Conservative Party* after 1918. In power 1924 and 1929–31, when it split over Ramsay MacDonald's decision to form a National Government with the Conservatives and Liberals. In government 1945–51, 1964–70, 1974–79 and 1997 to date; in the latter case, as 'New Labour', adopted many of the values of Margaret Thatcher to appeal to middle-class voters.

Liberalism   A belief in individual liberty, tolerance of diversity (at home and abroad) and limiting the powers of government.

Liberal Party   Founded 1859 (see *Peelites*). Held power in Britain 1868–74, 1880–85, 1886, 1892–95 and 1906–16. Split under the pressures of the First World War and replaced as the 'alternative party of government' to the *Tories* by *Labour*. In 1988 renamed as the *Liberal Democrats* following merger with the Social Democratic Party (founded 1981 by liberal-minded defectors from Labour).

Marshall Aid   US-financed programme to promote the economic recovery of Western Europe, 1948–51. Named after US Secretary of State George Marshall.

Nationalism   The consciousness of 'distinctiveness' of people sharing a language, territory or culture. In the twentieth century, it underlay many of the struggles by colonised peoples against their imperial overlords and re-emerged both in many parts of the former Soviet bloc and in parts of Western Europe (e.g. Flanders) in the 1990s.

NATO   North Atlantic Treaty Organisation: framework for military cooperation between the USA and Western European countries, established in 1949 to counter the Soviet 'threat'. In recent years has broadened its sphere of operations, e.g. against the Taliban (Islamic fundamentalists) in Afghanistan.

Oligarchy   Government by an unelected and self-perpetuating elite.

Peelites   MPs who remained loyal to Peel after the 1846 split among the *Tories*. Returned to government in the 1852 Aberdeen Coalition and joined with the *Whigs* and *Radicals* to form the *Liberal Party* in 1859.

Protestant Ascendancy   Rule over Ireland by a *Protestant* (mainly English) *gentry* class. Started in the early seventeenth century, but fully implemented only after 1689.

Radicals   Emerged in Britain in the 1820s as supporters of universal manhood suffrage. Continued as the left-wing of the *Liberal Party* down to the First World War.

Raj   British rule in India from 1858 to 1947.

Realpolitik   Policy (especially foreign) devoid of ethical considerations.

Reich   German for 'Empire'. The First Reich was the Holy Roman Empire (800–1806), the Second, Wilhelmine Germany (1870–1918), the Third, Nazi Germany (1933–45).

Sanctions   Economic measures (such as restricting the flow of oil or capital) imposed to make 'rogue' countries obey internationally agreed norms, e.g. against Italy in the 1930s, Southern Rhodesia in the 1960s, Iraq in the 1990s and Iran in the early twenty-first century.

Scramble for Africa   The partitioning of Africa by European powers (Britain, France, Belgium, Italy, Portugal and Germany) after 1870, reflecting both a desire for new markets and sources of raw materials and the extension of European rivalries to the 'dark continent'. The process of partition was formalised by the Congress of Berlin (1884–85), but this did not prevent territorial disputes between the powers developing on occasion into major international confrontations. The colonial boundaries drawn up by the Europeans took little account of African tribal divisions, creating artificial political units that inevitably proved extremely unstable after independence.

Sinn Fein   'Ourselves Alone' (*Gaelic*). Irish nationalist party founded by Arthur Griffith, 1906. Won a majority of Irish seats in the 1918 general election; set up the *Dail Eireann* (Irish parliament) and declared independence in 1919. Split over the 1921 Anglo-Irish Agreement (which set up the Irish Free State) and thereafter insignificant until it emerged as the political wing of the IRA in the 1970s. Since 2007 shares power in Northern Ireland with the Democratic Unionists (a hard-line Protestant party founded by the Reverend Ian Paisley in 1971).

Socialism   A belief in an egalitarian society where the means of production and exchange are owned by the community and run for the common good.

Sovereignty   The locus of power in a state. In Britain, resides in Crown and Parliament, in the USA in 'the people'.

Spin   PR in politics: a term coined after 1997. However, this form of manipulation of the news media, aimed primarily at a domestic audience, has been used in Britain since (at least) the 1790s.

Suffrage   Synonym for *franchise*.

Syndicalism   From *syndicat* (*Fr*): a belief that industry should be run by the trade unions. Popular in France, the USA and the UK in the early twentieth century: in the British case led to the movement for amalgamation of unions to form stronger organisations and the labour unrest of 1910–14.

Terrorism   An attempt to achieve political ends by inflicting injury or death on innocent members of the civilian population. Associated particularly with the later twentieth century (e.g. in Ireland, in the Middle East and, above all, with 9/11) it should be distinguished from *guerrilla warfare* – attacks on occupying forces by troops, usually not uniformed and indistinguishable from the host population.

Tories   Irish bandits: a name given to supporters of Charles II by the *Whigs* and still popularly used to describe the Conservative Party.

Total War   The mobilisation of all the resources of the State (human and economic) in the prosecution of war.

Totalitarianism   Where a single party controls (or attempts to control) all aspects of life. A twentieth-century term, associated with Nazi Germany, Fascist Italy and the Soviet Union: differs from *absolutism* in exercising control by all means at its disposal (e.g. the mass media) and in its sway over private life.

United Kingdom (UK)   Created by the 1800 Act of Union with Ireland. If writing on the eighteenth century (after the union with Scotland in 1707), 'Britain' should be used.

United Provinces   The official name of the Dutch Republic, 1588–1795: usually known as 'Holland', although this was only one of the seven provinces that made up the federation.

Warsaw Pact   Established 1955 by communist East European states as a response to *NATO*. It enabled the Soviet Union to reinforce its control over Eastern Europe and was used to justify the invasion of Hungary (1956) and Czechoslovakia (1968). Formally abolished 1991.

Welfare state   Phrase coined in the 1930s: the idea that the State should be responsible for the welfare of all its citizens, regardless of class or income, from cradle to grave. Although the origins of the British welfare state can be seen in the reforms of the *Liberal* Government before the First World War, its realisation had to await *Labour*'s implementation (1945–51) of the recommendations of the 1942 Beveridge Report.

Whigs   Originally a term of abuse directed at Scottish Presbyterian rebels. Used by the *Tories* for those late seventeenth-century

English politicians who believed in limiting the powers of the Crown, but rapidly adopted as the accepted label of the 'party' (in practice, often divided by bitter rivalries), which, from Walpole onwards, dominated eighteenth-century politics and, after eclipse in the 1780s, re-emerged as a major political force in the 1820s. Subsumed in the *Liberal Party* from 1859, 'Whiggism' remained an important (aristocratic) strand for some years, but disappeared after the 1880s, as many/most Whigs gravitated towards the *Conservative Party*.

Economic, social and cultural history

Agricultural Revolution   The introduction of new crops and techniques and the process of *enclosure*, encouraged by the great landowners. In Britain, conventionally placed in the eighteenth century. Modern views see this as oversimplified and stress rather the incremental process of change in farming (even in the *open field system*) from the early sixteenth to the mid-nineteenth century.

Anglican Church   Term employed since the mid-nineteenth century by the Church of England to describe itself. Historians often use it more widely for the C. of E. from the Restoration (1660) onwards. As a result of nineteenth-century missionary activity, there is also a worldwide *Anglican Communion* (which includes the Episcopalian Church in the USA) led by the Archbishop of Canterbury, but at the time of writing this appears on the verge of break-up (*schism*) over issues of human sexuality.

Aristocracy   The 'upper classes': the hereditary nobility, in Britain stretching from dukes down to baronets.

Arminianism   Named after the Dutch theologian, Jacob Arminius (1560–1609). A rejection of the doctrines of John Calvin, particularly *Predestination* (the belief that human beings are irrevocably divided from birth into the 'Elect' and the 'Damned'). In England, associated with William Laud (Archbishop of Canterbury, 1635–45), who attempted to restore elements of pre-*Reformation* liturgical practice: 'the beauty of holiness' opposed by the austere Calvinistic *Puritans*.

Balance of payments   The net surplus or deficit of a country's exports over its imports (in both cases including 'invisible' items such as capital flows).

Bretton Woods   Anglo-American economic conference, 1944, which established the International Monetary Fund (IMF) and World Bank.

Capitalism   An economic system in which property and the means of production are privately owned and dependent on market forces. Can co-exist – and in all developed capitalist economies does – with a greater or lesser degree of social welfare provision by the State.

Class   Emerged in the late eighteenth century as a label to indicate the relative positions of groups or individuals within society, with the corollary, drawn by Marx and Engels, that these have different or conflicting interests (see *Marxist interpretation of history*). In Britain, the 'official' model of social class (Classes I–V) was devised by the Registrar-General in 1911 and is still used (with modifications) by government today.

Conspicuous consumption   Spending ostentatiously to demonstrate one's position in society.

Counter-Reformation   The counter-attack on *Protestant* ideas launched by the Roman Catholic Church in the three sessions of the Council of Trent (1545–47, 1551–52, 1562–63) and led largely by the Jesuit order. Particularly successful in Poland, France and the Habsburg dominions.

Deism   School of thought prominent in seventeenth- and eighteenth-century Europe. Deists retained a belief in the existence of a God, but rejected Christianity in favour of 'natural religion' – the philosophical and ethical principles held in common by all religions.

Diocese   The area governed by a bishop. There were 17 dioceses in medieval England; a further five were created at the *Reformation* and 20 since 1836.

Dissent/Nonconformity   Dissent was a term applied from the mid-seventeenth century to those (e.g. Baptists, Independents and Quakers) who refused to belong to the Church of England (and were granted formal toleration in 1689). In the eighteenth century, 'New Dissent' emerged as a result of the *Evangelical Revival*, the most prominent movement being Wesleyan Methodism (and its offshoots). In the nineteenth century, *Nonconformity* became the generally used label and remains so today.

Domestic/putting-out system(s)   Manufacturing in which the unit of production is the household (e.g. the East Anglian textile industry before 1800). The illusion of independence this gave was just that: increasingly workers owned nothing but their skills and their time as work was 'put out' by capitalist merchants, who owned both the material and the machines (e.g. looms).

Embourgeoisement   Adoption of middle-class values and lifestyles by those immediately below them.

Enclosure/Inclosure   The process by which the *open fields* and common land that covered much of south and east England in the late Middle Ages were taken into private occupation. Until about 1730, most enclosure was either by agreement between individual landowners, or carried out by a single landlord in a parish he controlled. Thereafter, enclosure by Act of Parliament became the norm: the peak years were between 1793 and 1815, under the pressure to make maximum use of land when grain prices reached record heights during the Revolutionary and Napoleonic Wars. 'Inclosure' is the term preferred by archivists.

Enlightenment   Eighteenth-century intellectual movement in Western Europe (especially France) that emphasised 'reason' as the criterion for social and political improvement.

Eugenics   A quasi-scientific belief, popular from the late nineteenth century and deriving from *Social Darwinism*, that the nation's stock should or could be improved by encouraging the healthier and more intelligent to reproduce and discouraging (or preventing) those less fortunate from doing so. Popular across the political spectrum in early twentieth-century Britain, but rapidly abandoned by most of its adherents with the rise of Nazi Germany.

Evangelical Revival   An eighteenth-century religious movement that affected all *Protestant* countries but was particularly marked in Britain and the American colonies (where it was known as the *Great Awakening*). Evangelicals stressed the individual's direct relationship with God (achieved through a conversion experience) and the literal truth of the Bible. They were very prominent in British political life and humanitarian movements between 1790 and 1850.

Feudalism   The basis of economy and society in medieval Europe. In essence, the mutual obligations of vassals and their superiors (from the humblest peasant to the monarch), linked by the granting of land in return for services such as labour or military service.

Free trade   First fully expounded by Adam Smith in *The Wealth of Nations* (1776): the principle that imports and exports should flow freely between countries without tariff barriers for the good of both producers and consumers.

Gentry   English landowners ranking below the *aristocracy*: 'knights', esquires' and 'gentlemen'. Prominent from the sixteenth to the late nineteenth century in local government as magistrates and in national politics as MPs.

Gold standard   The value of a currency in relation to a quantity of gold and therefore determining the exchange rate between them. By the late nineteenth century, virtually universal among trading nations, but abandoned in the First World War. Attempts to return to it thereafter were a contributory (and in Britain a major) factor in exacerbating world economic problems, and it was abandoned in 1931.

Husbandmen   Early modern English tenant farmers, with 10–30 acres.

Indulgences   The remission of penalties for sins in return for payment or 'good works' in late medieval Europe. Luther's 1517 attack on the practice sparked off the *Reformation*.

Industrial archaeology   A stepchild of history and archaeology, born in the 1950s. Originally concerning itself with the technologies and physical survivals of the *Industrial Revolution* and the Railway Age, in recent years it has encompassed areas as diverse as council houses, supermarkets and nuclear bunkers. Much of the early leg-work was performed by 'amateurs', hence perhaps the reluctance of many professional historians until recently to recognise its value.

Industrial Revolution   Originally applied by the French historian, Jérôme Blanqui, in 1839 to the transformation of the British economy between 1780 and 1830 through coal, iron and cotton. Refined by later nineteenth-century scholars (such as Arnold Toynbee) and applied to other countries, such as the *post-bellum* USA, the concept came under attack from the 1920s by others who believed that the transformation in Britain was less dramatic than previously believed, that capital-intensive industries had existed since the sixteenth century and that elements of continuity in the economy were at least as strong as those of change. The controversy continues. (See also *Second Industrial Revolution*.)

Keynesianism   Economic theory advanced by the Cambridge economist, John Maynard Keynes (1883–1946), and given fullest expression in his *General Theory of Employment, Interest and Money* (1936). Governments can ensure full employment by deficit financing (i.e. spending above their means) to maintain demand and thus full employment. It underlay British economic policy 1945–79, until replaced by *monetarism* under Margaret Thatcher.

Labour aristocracy   In nineteenth-century Britain, skilled (and thus more highly paid) workers, usually in the newer industries (e.g. shipbuilding, engineering, the railways). Much of the pre-1867 debate over Parliamentary reform revolved around how they could be identified and thus enfranchised.

Laissez-faire   Minimal state interference in economic and social life.

Mercantilism   The prevailing economic orthodoxy of the seventeenth and eighteenth centuries, it stressed the importance of a favourable balance of trade: one country could only benefit at the expense of another. Trade thus had to be regulated (in England by the 'Navigation Laws', 1651–96), domestic manufacturers protected against foreign, and colonies acquired as a source of raw materials and as captive markets.

Monetarism   A post-1960 reaction to *Keynesianism*, which right-wing economists saw as leading inexorably to inflation. Adopted in Britain (*Thatcherism*) and the USA (*Reaganomics*) in the 1980s, it saw strict control of the money supply as the means of ensuring economic stability.

National debt   Money that governments owe as a consequence of taking out loans.

Open field system   Medieval/early modern farming system. Unhedged and very large fields (at least three per parish) were divided into strips (*selions*). One field would lie fallow each year to recover its fertility and allow common grazing. Parishioners also had grazing rights on common pasture (strictly limited) and 'waste' (low-quality land). Widespread over much of Western Europe.

Oxford Movement   A perception by 'high church' *Anglicans* from the 1830s that much of the historical and spiritual legacy of the Church had been lost at the *Reformation*. Ideas were spread by a series of pamphlets known as *Tracts for the Times*, hence supporters are sometimes known as *Tractarians* or (after one of the most prominent) *Puseyites*. Several leading members (e.g. John Henry Newman and Henry Manning) converted to Roman Catholicism in the 1840s/1850s, but many of the practices that the movement advocated (e.g. wearing vestments, chanting Psalms) had become part of mainstream Anglicanism by 1900 and remain so today.

Pays   Literally 'country' (*Fr*). A synonym for *region*: what distinguishes culturally, socially and linguistically one part of a country from another and gives its inhabitants a sense of shared identity and (arguably) a common history.

Pre-industrial   Describes an economy in which the majority of the population derive their livelihood from activities other than factory-based industry. Usually applied to England between 1500 and 1780. Importantly, does not mean an economy without industry, but one where this is organised largely on *domestic/ putting-out system(s)*.

Protectionism   Defending, by means of tariff barriers, a country's industries from those of its rivals. Contrast *free trade*.

Protestantism   Emerged in the sixteenth century from the writings of Martin Luther and John Calvin. Sees the Bible as the only source of truth; justification (salvation) can only come through faith, rather than 'good works' (see *Indulgences*).

Proto-industrialisation   An alternative label for *pre-industrial*; stresses the importance of the *domestic/putting-out system(s)* in building up the capital and entrepreneurial skills essential for 'proper' (i.e. factory-based) industrialisation.

Reformation   The sixteenth-century schism in western Christendom as a result of the spread of *Protestant* ideas. Some historians argue that a Catholic reformation was in progress before the split.

Renaissance   Literally 're-birth': the fourteenth- to sixteenth-century revival of interest (starting in Italy) in the ideas of classical antiquity.

Second Industrial Revolution   The transformation of much of the western world between 1870 and 1914 as a result of the application of science and techniques of mass production to industrial processes, in areas such as steel, chemicals, electricity and the internal combustion engine.

Secularisation   The twentieth-century waning, at least in Western Europe, of Christian beliefs and observance as the basis of society, culture and political adherence.

Social Darwinism   The late nineteenth-century application of the principle of Darwinian natural selection to political and social analysis. Although most frequently used to support competitive individualism and *laissez-faire* ideas (and *Eugenics*), it also contributed to the *Liberal* welfare reforms of 1906–14.

Yeomen   Small landowners or prosperous tenant farmers. The bedrock of early modern English villages: they provided employment and ran local government as churchwardens, constables and jurors.

Varieties of history and historical writing

Anachronism   Using concepts and language alien to the period under discussion.

Annales School   Named after the influential journal *Annales d'histoire économique et social*, founded by the French historians Lucien Febvre and Marc Bloch in 1929 and distinguished by its *interdisciplinarity*. Revolutionary at the time, e.g. in its use of concepts drawn from sociology and (especially) cultural geography, it is today an accepted and essential part of the historian's toolkit.

Cliometrics   A term coined in the 1960s for the 'quantitative' approach to history. It involves testing common historical assumptions against available or (more often and more controversially) inferred statistics, often to investigate *counter-factual* questions. 'Clio' is the Greek goddess of history; 'metrics' means measurement.

Comparative history   An approach to historical study that believes insights can be gained by comparing and contrasting societies, institutions and structures. It has perhaps been most fruitfully applied to the study of *totalitarian* regimes, especially Hitler's Germany and Stalin's USSR.

Contemporary history   The history of the recent past. Incapable of precise definition: originally coined for the period since 1945, to distinguish this from 'modern' history (since 1815).

Counterfactual history   What would have happened if . . .?

Determinism   The view that history is governed ('determined') by forces other than the motives and actions of individuals, for example geography or technology.

Dialectic/dialectic materialism   Derived from the German philosopher, G.W.F. Hegel, and used by Marx to explain how economies (the 'substructure') and their political and social institutions (the 'superstructure') develop: the struggle between 'thesis' and 'antithesis' being resolved in 'synthesis'.

Historicism   The belief that historical study can reveal general laws of social development.

Historiography   The history and study of historical writing.

Ideology   A body of ideas. A *dominant ideology* is one that determines social and political norms.

Interdisciplinarity   Scholarship that makes use of the concepts and methodology of academic disciplines other than history.

Marxist interpretation of history   The belief that the struggle between social classes is the key to understanding history. Produced some of the best (and worst) historical writing of the twentieth century.

Medieval   Broadly, the period between the eleventh century and the *Reformation*, although some British historians extend it down to 1558 or even 1603.

Objectivity   Attempting a value-free and dispassionate view of the past and thus related to *positivism* (2).

Positivism   (1) Social theory derived from the writings of the nineteenth-century French philosopher, Auguste Comte, who believed a 'religion of humanity' based on shared moral values could be achieved without metaphysical or theological under-pinnings. Very influential in the later nineteenth century; George Eliot is perhaps its best-known British adherent. (2) Using the methods of the natural and social sciences in history to reach conclusions free from value judgements.

Revisionism   A compulsive tendency among historians to challenge the ideas of their predecessors, usually in the light of either prevailing political ideologies or the need to keep themselves in employment.

Value judgement   A verdict on the past influenced by the moral, religious, cultural or social values of the historian.

Whig interpretation of history   Historical writing that sees the past in terms of 'progress' towards the present day.

The British monetary system before decimalisation

Unless you're a (very) mature student you will have no first-hand knowledge of the pre-1971 monetary system.

As today, the basic unit was the pound sterling (£), which was divided into 20 shillings (written 's') and 240 pence (written 'd', from the Latin *denarius*). Pounds, shillings and pence were usually separated (in informal writing, e.g. a letter) by a forward-slash: thus 12/6 (12 shillings and 6 pence); 12 shillings exactly would be written 12/-, not 12/0. In advertisements, catalogues and the like the longer form 12s 6d would be more normal. Prices below about £10 were almost invariably quoted in shillings/pence: thus '60/-' rather than '£3'.

As an added complication there was a further unit, the guinea. This equated to 21 shillings and was commonly used for profes-sional fees (e.g. by lawyers) and is still used today for some major horseraces (e.g. the 2,000 Guineas at Newmarket).

The commonly-used notes and coins were:

Notes

Pound (£)	Originally the gold sovereign; withdrawn in 1914.
Ten shillings (10/-)	Commonly called 'ten bob'.

'Silver' (in practice, no silver content post-1947)

Half-crown (2/6)	Under the influence of Hollywood, often called 'half a dollar' after *c*.1925.
Florin (2/-)	Commonly called 'two bob'.
Shilling (1/-)	Known as the 'bob'.
Sixpence (6d)	Known as the 'tanner'.

'Copper'

Threepence (3d)	Known, at least in Yorkshire, as the 'joey' (silver threepenny [pronounced 'thrupny'] pieces remained in circulation until the 1950s).
Penny (1d)	Often known as the 'copper', as in 'Spare a copper, Guv?'
Halfpenny (½d)	Pronounced 'haypenny'.
Farthing (¼d)	

In modern terms, 'ten bob' equates to the 50p piece, the florin to 10p and the shilling to 5p. Such conversions are, however, meaningless in terms of purchasing power.

The Christian year

From early medieval times to the nineteenth century the lives of most Western European people were regulated by the religious calendar. This gave them both holidays (especially Patronal Festivals – the feast of the saint after whom the local parish church was named and often called *wakes*) and a legal and agricultural framework to the year. Many had been grafted by the early Christian Church onto earlier pagan celebrations. The most important fixed dates (and their significance, at least in England) were:

6 January	Epiphany (Twelfth Night): end of the traditional Christmas holiday; when work started again on the land.
2 February	Candlemas: before the Reformation, mothers who had given birth in the preceding year took candles to church as a thanksgiving for safe delivery. In some areas (e.g. Hardy's Wessex) when annual hiring fairs were held for farm labourers looking for new places (elsewhere, these were in October).
14 February	St Valentine: if you were a girl and had placed bay leaves under your pillow on the night of the 13th, the first person (of the opposite sex) you would see would be a potential sweetheart.
1 March	St David: patron saint of Wales.
17 March	St Patrick: patron saint of Ireland.
25 March	Assumption of the Blessed Virgin Mary (Lady Day): New Year's Day until 1752, when Britain adopted the Gregorian calendar.
23 April	St George: patron saint of England.
1 August	Lammas Day: the start of harvest and also of common grazing in the open fields. High-quality permanent pasture was often thus known as 'Lammas lands'. From 1753, 13 August.

29 September	Michaelmas: traditionally the end of the farming and accounting years. In many areas, the major time for fairs and animal sales.
31 October	All Souls' Eve (Hallowe'en): many customs and beliefs attached to it. In rural Yorkshire it was believed, at least until the 1870s, that an overnight vigil in a church porch would reveal to the 'wise' the souls of those who would die in the coming year.
1 November	All Saints' Day.
2 November	All Souls' Day: commemoration of the souls of the departed.
30 November	St Andrew: patron saint of Scotland.
Sunday after 30 November	Advent Sunday: begins the ecclesiastical year.
25 December	Christmas Day.

Additionally, there were/are movable feasts, dependent on the phases of the Moon. These are, in chronological order:

Ash Wednesday	Beginning of Lent (the next 40 days).
Mothering Sunday	Apprentices and domestic servants were allowed the day off to visit their mothers. Today, Americanised to 'Mothers' Day'.
Palm Sunday	Entry of Christ into Jerusalem.
Maundy Thursday	The Last Supper.
Good Friday	Crucifixion of Christ.
Easter Day	Resurrection of Christ.
Rogation Sunday	Also Plough Sunday: prayers for a good harvest, often accompanied by processions around the fields and the parish boundaries.
Ascension Day	Ascension of Christ into Heaven.

Whitsunday	Descent of the Holy Spirit on the Apostles. Generally a celebration of Spring: maypoles and much fun behind the church.
Trinity Sunday	Celebration of the Holy Trinity (Father, Son and Holy Spirit). Traditionally the start of the hay harvest.

There is also one twentieth-century innovation:

Remembrance Sunday	The Sunday after 11 November, 'Armistice Day', which ended the First World War on 'the eleventh hour of the eleventh day of the eleventh month'. Instituted 1919 to commemorate the Fallen; today embraces all who have died in subsequent conflicts.

Index

Reading Primary Sources
The Interpretation of Texts from 19th and 20th Century History

Miriam Dobson and Benjamin Ziemann

Reading Primary Sources is at once a bold and useful book
... With felicity and insight, the authors of this volume
show us how modern historians now read primary sources
... A wonderful volume for teachers and students alike.
Helmut Walser Smith,
Vanderbilt University, USA

Finally, a text that puts theory into practice! *Reading Primary Sources* will
help students to understand key concepts in historical analysis and recent
historiographical trends and guide them in the analysis of various genres
of historical texts.

Caroline Hoefferle,
Wingate University, USA

Primary sources are not only the very basis of historical research, but are also
widely used in undergraduate teaching as a way to introduce students to
voices from the past. The contributors to this book explore various traditions
in source-criticism, explain the different ways documents can be read, and
use exciting examples from their own research to suggest the insights (and
also difficulties) texts might offer.

Taking into account the huge expansion in the range of primary sources
used by historians, the volume includes chapters on opinion polls, surveil-
lance reports, testimony, and court files in addition to more traditional genres
such as letters, memoranda, diaries, novels, newspapers, political speeches,
and autobiography. To aid the reader's understanding of source criticism,
the chapters in the first part of this unique volume give an overview of both
traditional and new methodological approaches to the use of primary
documents. In addition, the introduction offers an accessible checklist suggesting some of the most important steps for interpreting historical sources.

Taking examples of sources from many European countries and the USA,
and providing up-to-date information on the most widely used textual
sources, this is the perfect companion for every student of history who wants
to engage with primary sources.

ISBN13: 978–0–415–42956–6 (hbk)
ISBN13: 978–0–415–42957–3 (pbk)
ISBN13: 978–0–203–89221–3 (ebk)

For ordering and further information please visit:
www.routledge.com

The Modern Historiography Reader

Western Sources

Edited by Adam Budd

Historiography – the history of historical writing – is one of the most important and basic areas of study for all historians. Yet in such a broad and expanding field, how should students find their way through it?

In *The Modern Historiography Reader: Western Sources*, Adam Budd guides readers through European and North American developments in history-writing since the eighteenth century. Starting with Enlightenment history and moving through subjects such as moral history, national history, the emergence of history as a profession, and the impact of scientific principles on history, he then looks at some of the most important developments in twentieth-century historiography such as social history, traumatic memory, postcolonialism, gender history, postmodernism, and the history of material objects.

This is the only book that brings together historiographical writing from anthropology, literary theory, philosophy, psychology, and sociology – as well as history. Each of the thirteen thematic sections begins with a clear introduction that familiarizes readers with the topics and articles, setting them in their wider contexts. They explain what historiography is, how historians' perspectives and sources determine the kinds of questions they ask, and discuss how social and ideological developments have shaped historical writing over the past three centuries.

With a glossary of critical terms and reading lists for each section, *The Modern Historiography Reader: Western Sources* is the perfect introduction to modern historiography.

ISBN13: 978–0–415–45886–3 (hbk)
ISBN13: 978–0–415–45887–0 (pbk)

For ordering and further information please visit:
www.routledge.com

Sceptical History
Feminist and Postmodern Approaches in Practice

Hélène Bowen Raddeker

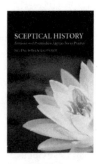

'One of the great virtues of the book is that it uses examples from historical writing worldwide, examining global subjects ... The book is clearly written and full of insights about a wide range of historical topics. It is a welcome handbook for both teachers and students, even for advanced historians who want to know more about postmodern theory.'

Bonnie Smith, *Rutgers University*

Sceptical History familiarises readers with the postmodern critique of history whilst also focusing upon the question of how to practise postmodernist feminist (sceptical) history.

A highly original work, this book considers major themes including cultural, class and sexual identity and 'difference', weaving them into debates on the nature and methods of history. In so doing it arrives at new ways of doing 'history and theory' that do not exclude feminist approaches or attention to non-Western history.

Hélène Bowen Raddeker's arguments extend beyond the postmodernist critique of history to other aspects of postmodernist thinking, including the postcolonial challenge to humanism and Eurocentric metanarratives of progress. Using a wide range of historical and cultural examples, she draws extensively on feminist scholarship and historiography.

Sceptical History provides an accessible guide to some of the most complex theories current today.

ISBN13: 978–0–415–34115–8 (hbk)
ISBN13: 978–0–415–34114–1 (pbk)
ISBN13: 978–0–203–47916–2 (ebk)

Available at all good bookshops
For ordering and further information please visit:
www.routledge.com

Practicing History
New Directions in Historical Writing After the Linguistic Turn

Edited by Gabrielle M. Spiegel

This essential new collection of key articles examines the current status of the debate over the linguistic turn and rethinks the practice of history in light of its implications, attempting to move beyond its initial formulation and reception. Written by a mix of critical thinkers and practicing historians, this is an indispensable survey of current ideas and a timely read.

ISBN13: 978–0–415–34107–3 (hbk)
ISBN13: 978–0–415–34108–0 (pbk)
ISBN13: 978–0–203–33569–7 (ebk)

What is History For?

Beverley Southgate

'An essential read ... this is an informed scholarly and lucidly written text on the purposes of history which also confronts the inadequate shibboleths of today's dominant 'history culture'.

Professor Keith Jenkins,
University College, Chichester

'Beverly Southgate has an elegant and open style that is an excellent vehicle for getting complex ideas across'.

Professor Alun Munslow,
University of Staffordshire

What is History For? is a timely publication that examines the purpose and point of historical studies. Recent debates on the role of the humanities and the ongoing impact of post-structuralist thought on the very nature of historical enquiry, have rendered the question of what history is for of utmost importance.

Charting the development of historical studies, Beverley Southgate examines the various uses to which history has been put. While history has often supposedly been studied 'for its own sake', Southgate argues that this seemingly innocent approach masks an inherent conservatism and exposes the ways in which history has, sometimes deliberately, sometimes inadvertently, been used for socio-political purposes. This fascinating historicisation of the study of history is unique in its focus on the future of the subject as well as its past, and provides compulsive reading for students and the general reader alike.

ISBN13: 978–0–415–35098–3 (hbk)
ISBN13: 978–0–415–35099–0 (pbk)
ISBN13: 978–0–203–69666–8 (ebk)

History: What and Why?

Beverley Southgate

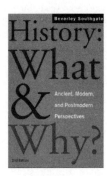

History: What and Why? is an introductory survey of the nature and purpose of history.

Beverley Southgate argues that the traditional model of the subject as a re-discovery of the past 'as it was' has now been superseded. It has been successfully challenged by developments in other disciplines, such as linguistics, psychology and philosophy, together with the work of Marxist, feminist and post-colonial historians.

This book combines a historical perspective with a clear guide to current debates about the nature of history. It proposes a positive role for historical study in the postmodern era.

ISBN13: 987–0–415–25657–5 (hbk)
ISBN13: 978–0–415–25658–2 (pbk)
ISBN13: 978–0–203–93016–8 (ebk)

The Routledge Companion to Historical Studies

Alun Munslow

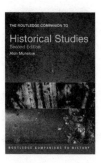

The Routledge Companion to Historical Studies serves as a much needed critical introduction to the key issues, historians, philosophers and theories which have prompted the rethinking of history and its practice that has gathered pace since the 1990s.

Key concepts that address both how historians work and organise the past, such as class, empiricism, agency/structure, epistemology, and hermeneutics are examined through the ideas of leading historians and philosophers such as Vico, Croce, Collingwood, Elton, Kant, Nietzsche, Derrida, and White. Many entries have been substantially updated and offer an essential analysis of the state of history thinking and practice today. Alun Munslow has added 29 new entries including Carl Becker, Frank R. Ankersmit, Richard Rorty, Jean-Francois Lyotard, Jean Baudrillard, gender, justified belief, the aesthetic turn, race, film, biography, cultural history, critical theory and experimental history.

With a revised introduction setting out the state of the discipline of history today, as well as an extended and updated bibliography, *The Routledge Companion to Historical Studies* is the essential reference work for all students of history.

ISBN13: 978–0–415–38576–3 (hbk)
ISBN13: 978–0–415–38577–0 (pbk)
ISBN13: 978–0–203–96996–0 (ebk)

Philosophy of History

M.C. Lemon

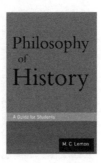

Philosophy of History is an essential introduction to a vast body of writing about history, from Classical Greece and Rome to the contemporary world. M.C. Lemon maps out key debates and central concepts of philosophy of history, placing principal thinkers in the context of their times and schools of thought.

Lemon explains the crucial differences between *speculative* philosophy as an enquiry into the course and meaning of history, and *analytic* philosophy of history as relating to the nature and methods of history as a discipline. Divided into three parts this guide provides a comprehensive study of history thought since ancient times.

ISBN13: 978–0–415–16204–3 (hbk)
ISBN13: 978–0–415–16205–0 (pbk)
ISBN13: 978–0–203–38023–9 (ebk)